Understanding People

or

How to Be Your Very Own Shrink

Understanding People

or

How to Be Your Very Own Shrink

Julie Rogers, Ph. D.

Nelson-Hall nh Chicago

Library of Congress Cataloging in Publication Data

Rogers, Julie.
   Understanding people.

   Bibliography: p.

    1. Counseling.   2. Helping behavior.   3. Humanistic
psychology.   I.   Title.
BF637.C6R63   158   78-31175
ISBN 0-88229-273-0 **(cloth)**
ISBN 0-88229-678-7 **(paper)**

Manufactured in the United States of America

10   9   8   7   6   5   4   3   2   1

Table of Contents

Acknowledgments

I want to express my sincere gratitude to all my Humanistic Psychology Institute friends, whose gentle philosophy forms the foundation of this book.

I am also deeply obligated to Dr. Josephine Chandler, professor emeritus of San Jose State University, who inspired her students to develop a sensitivity to all functions of the English language.

Please Hear
What I'm Not Saying*

Don't be fooled by me. Don't be fooled by the face I wear. For I wear a thousand masks, masks that I'm afraid to take off, and none of them are me. Pretending is an art that's second nature with me, but don't be fooled. My surface may seem smooth, but my surface is my mask. Beneath dwells the real me in confusion, fear, and loneliness. But I hide this and panic at the fear of being exposed. That's why I frantically create a mask to hide behind, a nonchalant, sophisticated facade, to help me pretend, to shield me from the glance that

*From *Masks* by Peter Lehmann. Copyright © 1974 by Celestial Arts. Reprinted with permission of Celestial Arts (231 Adrian Road, Millbrae, California, 94030) publisher.

knows. But such a glance is precisely my salvation, and I know it. That is, if it is followed by acceptance and love. It's the only thing that will assure me of what I can't assure myself, that I am worth something. But I don't dare tell you this. I'm afraid to. I'm afraid you'll think less of me, that you'll laugh at me. And your laugh would kill me. I'm afraid that deep down I'm no good, I'm nothing, and that you'll see this and reject me. So I play my game, my desperate game, with a facade of assurance without and a trembling child within. And so begins the parade of masks. I chatter to you in suave tones of surface talk. I tell you everything that is really nothing, and nothing that is really everything—of what's crying within me. So please listen carefully and hear what I'm not saying, what for survival I need to say, but what I can't say. I dislike hiding. Honestly, I'd like to be genuine and spontaneous and me. But you've got to help me. You've got to hold out your hand, even when that seems to be the last thing I want. Each time you've been kind and gentle, my heart grows wings. With your sensitivity and sympathy, you can breathe life into me. I want you to know how important you are to me, how you can be the creator of the person that is me, if you choose to. Please choose to. You alone can break down the wall behind which I tremble. Do not pass me by. *Please. Do not pass me by!* It will not be easy for you. A long conviction of worthlessness builds strong walls. The nearer you approach me, the blinder I strike back. I fight the very thing I cry out for. But I am told that love is stronger than walls and in this lies my hope. Who am I, you may wonder. I am someone you know very well. For I am *every man and every woman you meet.*

1.

What This Book Is All About

This book has been designed for you. That is, it has been designed for you if you want to learn to feel self-confident and free. Or if you have spent most of your life as an approval-seeking doormat, but now you want to learn how to say no and accept no without feeling guilt or fear. Or if you want to learn to go about problem solving in a simple, systematic manner.

Perhaps you want to understand other people so that you can interact and communicate harmoniously and happily, whether it be with fellow employees, friends, or relatives. Most persons find that when they understand human behavior and communication skills, they make friends easily and people their world with interesting, exciting companions of their own choosing, suited to their own particular needs and lifestyles.

1

In addition, you may want to learn how to serve as a "people-helper"[1] when other people come to you with their troubles. No matter who you are, where you live, what you do with your life, you cannot avoid listening sometimes to grievances or problems, or becoming aware of another human being's deep need to feel better about himself. You may counsel deliberately as a member of a volunteer organization or as an empathetic friend. Or you may do it casually, almost unmindfully, in the course of your daily life, just because you are a loving, concerned person. If you are a loyal friend, a spouse, a teacher, a bartender, a barber, a hair dresser, a coach, a policeman, a probation officer, or a boss, you need all the insights you can get, because you're bound to be a "people-helper," in one sense a counselor, like it or not. Parents are counselors the moment they take a tiny baby into their arms to make him feel safe and secure, and are often awe-stricken to think of the task before them. For the next eighteen years, more or less, they will serve as chief source of comfort and consolation, building a measure of security and self-esteem. Teachers also serve as counselors, "in loco parentis," as do grandparents and other relatives. As time goes on the sphere of influence upon the child widens until eventually it includes not only the peer group, but just about every possible contact—doctors, nurses, waitresses, beach-combers, post-men, disc jockeys, movie stars, TV repairmen and grocery clerks.

Of course, the licensed professionals, the real experts in the field, should be called upon to untangle the more severe emotional knots. No amateur should take it upon himself to play psychologist when the troubled person obviously requires highly trained, experienced attention. But the fact remains that most people go through life struggling to find their own way through the jungle of human relationships, confiding their worries to friends, parents, bartenders, and so on. It is an accepted fact that never in history has man suffered such perplexities in his effort to "get his head on straight." The fourteen to thirty-year-olds endure the biggest chunk of this frustration, but no age group is immune to the plagues of confusion and anxiety.

Growing up is painful even in the best of times and for most people it takes much of a lifetime to attain maturity. Each of us, like Adam and Eve, enacts the Garden of Eden story. Infancy is a time of blissful innocence. Then we gradually attain awareness, and at some point must leave the protective garden of ignorance. Invariably, like Adam and Eve, we find the world a place of "thorns and thistles." Like that first couple, we are not only compelled to face the fact of death, but must learn to handle our own and others' anger, jealousy, contempt, fear, and other sundry human emotions. Unlike our earliest forbears, we must also fit ourselves into structured economic and social systems. If we make this complicated adjustment somewhat successfully, without injuring ourselves or those around us, we have attained a degree of emotional maturity—a minor miracle!

Today emotional maturity is more difficult than ever, not only because of changing values and other complications, but because many of the former sources of emotional support have been withdrawn by our revised pattern of life. Before the days of transistor radio, TV, and a glut of recreational activities, the pastimes of reading and conversation filled the greatest portion of leisure time. Both of these help a person to grow and to find out who he is. This is especially true of the kind of conversation which gets down to the foundations of how people feel and think. Dr. Carl Rogers has built a whole psychology upon the principle that there is great therapeutic value in talking out one's mind to an accepting, nonjudgmental person, even though that person makes almost no comment in return. Verbalization ventilates the emotions, clarifies thinking, and paves the way for the individual to see life clearly, solve his problems, and strengthen his ego. Today's world is like that cartoon which shows a few primitive men gathered in a circle chattering. A Stone Age onlooker comments, "They've all learned to talk, but no one's learned to listen."

In the past there were many people who were not only willing, but eager to listen. The average home housed three generations as well as miscellaneous unattached relatives. Grandparents, bachelor uncles, and maiden aunts were delighted to give an ear to the young people's (or anyone's) experiences, daydreams, and opinions. Much time was spent this way. The dinner hour was a sacred round table ritual where ideas were shared in spontaneous give-and-take. Professional people also had more time to listen. Discussing the patient's family problems, whether medical, emotional, financial, or imaginary was part of the family "doc's" routine chores. Like the physician, the minister or the lawyer as a matter of course served as a wise and sympathetic listener for a wide spectrum of troubles, opinions, and feelings. Teachers, school principals, friends, and casual acquaintances all devoted more hours to relaxed conversation, serving as sounding boards for one another. Young people, instead of gathering in crowded noisy youth centers as they do now, met in the snug quietness of their own homes. Here two or three close friends would meet to compare their inner hopes and fears, and to pledge mutual loyalties. Everyone expected friendships to last forever.

Nowadays in order to find listeners, people are forced to join groups, called "encounter" groups, or "T" groups, or "discussion groups"; there seems to be no other way. The average home resembles a track meet with breathless contestants racing to and from mechanical devices such as cars, TV sets, refrigerators, bicycles, telephones, or doorbells. Dinner is a wild game of musical chairs. As for the professional world, M.D.'s rush from one treatment room to the next. Each patient recites his symptoms with the speed demanded of a tobacco auctioneer, often interrupted by a telephone or intercom. Ministers' efficient secretaries screen out all but emergency appointments, and school counselors must each divide their time among upwards of 400 bewildered counselees and almost twice as many frantic parents.

Of course no one is unaware of present day lack of communication sickness. Playwrights, novelists, artists, psychologists, and philosophers have drummed out the "alienation" theme to a tiresome degree. But the suggested remedies, such as joining clubs or churches, usually produce only "lonely crowds."

This is not to say there is not a great deal of talking going on in our world. On the contrary, there is often a deafening cacophony of nervous, senseless chatter, a noisy plea for recognition. But there's not much listening. The art and the opportunity have about perished.

Those who seek emotional security are blocked not only by this vacuum of communication, but by other complexities of our age. Bruno Bettelheim has skillfully analyzed present conditions. In the past, a growing child's world of values was orderly and understandable. The home, school, community, church, government, entertainment world, news media, and peer group all mostly agreed upon how the funny game of life was to be played. There were political and religious differences here and there, but the basic laws were clear-cut and unquestioned. True, a few misfits cheated, and a few were known as "characters," and a few were renegades, but generally there was no question about what behavior was praised or punished, what attitudes were tolerable or intolerable, or what goals were worthy or worthless.

But all that has changed. Now there are practically no universally accepted standards. Young adults find their parents' moral axioms meaningless. "Crime never pays?" Todays' crime records prove otherwise. "Virtue is rewarded?" Ask the lonely girl not invited to the prom. "Honesty is the best policy?" College bookstores, operated not by students but by businessmen, do a brisk business in handbooks on how to cheat on exams. "Winning isn't everything?" Then why are coaches of losing high school teams fired? Often not even youngsters' parents can agree upon policy, and this inconsistency pops up over and over again each day, so that, to the child, the world appears chaotic, therefore undependable. Young people, indeed all people to some extent, are staggered and baffled by the lack of stability in their environment and by lack of standards by which they can prove their own worth. Their reactions vary. They may try to escape by means of drugs, or they may become hostile as would frightened, frustrated animals, or they may defend themselves with neuroses.

Many others besides Bettelheim are voicing concern. As

long ago as the ancient Greek civilization hell was defined as chaos, a state which invariably leads to mental and emotional disturbances. If there is no order, one has no control and can make no sensible choices. Nothing is predictable. Life is a senseless nightmare.

In an attempt to bring order out of chaos, modern man is forced to spend great effort creating his own world of values—selecting his own mode of life, deciding what makes his life meaningful and significant. He reaches out for help with this complicated task because he feels uncertain and insecure. He hungers for some assurance that his decisions are valid, that he will survive. He is like a mountain climber who expects the mountains to be firm granite but instead finds them to be sliding shale. He feels himself slipping backwards, clawing and scrambling. He needs support; he needs people who understand him, who know how to help him understand himself, perhaps people like you.

If you do not belong to a volunteer organization, you might wonder how and where your "people-helping" training would be of use. Opportunities occur every day if you know how to take advantage of them. There is hardly any conversation where you cannot help someone feel a little more secure, a little more worthy. Or you may bump into a situation very obviously crying out for real sensitivity and charity. Perhaps you are attending a social gathering, seated comfortably with your libation in hand, regaling your friends with your waggish joviality, when the doorbell interrupts and a couple enter the room. No, they don't just enter the room, they *assault* the room with their importance. They are overdressed, over-bejeweled, and overpowering. In the most obvious tank maneuvers of the conversation they call attention to their large house, car, and boat. Determined not to give up the battle until every shred of the evening's enjoyment has been demolished, they go on to describe in deadly detail their daughter's exclusive finishing school and their own costly world cruise.

The average person would either ignore them (the ultimate insult), or wait slyly for a chance to stab them with a well-sharpened verbal barb. However, with your awareness and know-how, you recognize their sorry problem and undertake to stanch the obvious bleeding of their egos. With patience you listen to their falderol and with gentle tact you protect their vanity, acknowledging all their wonderful attainments—the symbols of their fragile security. After all, lending support at a party to the emotionally infirm is much like helping a physically handicapped child on the playground; it's the tender, kindly thing to do. It's a chance to give inadequate human beings a bit of much needed assurance.

Perhaps you recall some time when you've had your turn at receiving just the right support or empathetic understanding when you've needed it, if not from parents, then from a friend, minister, instructor, or casual acquaintance. If you're honest, you'll probably admit that the school teachers you remember best are not the ones who taught you the most, but the ones who gave you encouragement and a feeling of self-worth. On a "back-to-school night" one teacher was approached by the mother of a hyperactive, talkative teenage girl whom most of the school personnel had pronounced unmanageable. The mother wailed, "I suppose you find Janice impossible! Everyone else does. What shall I do?" The teacher protested mildly, "Please, don't do anything. Just tell her that in the course of our pleasant conversation I told you I like her very much, which is the truth." Those five words sound downright silly in their simplicity, but from that time on, Janice's new quietness and concentration in that classroom was miraculous. Years later when they happened to meet, Janice confessed to her former teacher, "I can't tell you how much those words meant to me. I used to say them over and over to myself, 'I like her very much, I like her very much,' hanging onto them the way a little kid does his blanket. It was so wonderful to know that someone really wanted me, just the way I was."

From my brief examples you may falsely assume that helping people to help themselves is a very simple art to master, that one needs only to be comforting, agreeable, and kind—sort of a Boy Scout out of uniform. As frustrated parents and overwhelmed bartenders and heartbroken spouses can testify, that assumption is not true. As with most every kind of skill, to do a good job takes knowledge, maturity, and sensitivity.

One more word before I get into the real core of the book. Remember that you people who are nonprofessionals can, in some cases, have even more influence and build more support than can professionals. For one thing, there's the built-in fact that you are holding out a helping hand just because you consider the other person a worthwhile human being, worthy of a slice of your own life, your valuable time, and your loving heart. No one is buying your friendship or your services. That in itself is enormously supportive in a way which no professional can supplant. Further, as a parent, a friend, an employer, a volunteer worker, or whatever, you can treat each interaction with a very personal interest. Often the troubled person responds wonderfully to that kind of sincerity. And finally, there is the fact that you are, in most instances, within easy access so that your help is steadily ongoing, whether the problems are significant crises, run-of-the-mill disappointments, or the puzzling search for Self.

Naturally, a nonprofessional must be wise enough to recognize his limitations and to know when the troubled person's behavior indicates a serious emotional disturbance requiring an expert hand—and ear.

2.

Acceptance

Effective "people-helping," whether helping oneself or others, always begins with the important factor of Acceptance. We often hear the theory that if we can accept ourselves, we then find it easy to accept others. But what can a person do if he's always found it too difficult to accept himself? What can he do if he experiences feelings of insecurity and guilt and lack of self-worth? In actuality, acceptance is a kind of merry-go-round; you can get onto it almost anywhere and eventually arrive at the same spot. The person who finds it difficult to accept himself could begin with learning to accept other people.

Sometimes patients say to me, "Oh, I can accept other people all right; I'm critical only of myself." But then invariably, before going far into the session, they betray the fact that they're harboring considerable bitterness and resentment. Their judgmentalism, however heavily hidden, begins to leak out around the edges.

Most of these people do not know why they feel so disturbed by the behavior of others. However, with a little detective work they would find that whenever they are "bugged" by other people, some kind of threat to their own security is involved. There's some threat to their basic philosophies or to their egos, or to extensions of their egos with which they identify strongly. Or perhaps in some way they feel a loss of control, a loss which makes them feel less strong and secure.

For instance, why is an adult motorist so very annoyed when he is delayed at a stop sign by a slow-moving pedestrian, perhaps a teenager? Because for those few seconds the motorist is helpless. He's powerless to move until the shuffling, indifferent pedestrian allows him to do so. The motorist may use all sorts of excuses for his anger, such as being in a hurry, but actually the lost five or ten seconds is not going to make any difference in his life. His real anger is generated by his feeling that the pedestrian is, for those seconds, in control. Further, why is a parent so incensed when a child does something his own way instead of the exact way the parent has directed? Perhaps a small child sits in a different chair from the one indicated, or an older child wears her own choice of clothes or is slow about doing the dishes. Basically, parents are annoyed when they don't feel dominant; it makes them feel powerful to control another human being and so they feel weakened when this control is no longer present.

In addition, most people are upset by any threat to their deep convictions—their constructs. The reason is simple. If one construct is wrong, perhaps their view of the whole world is distorted and unreal, a most upsetting suggestion. Probably nothing has engendered as much argument between fathers and sons as the dissimilar attitudes toward hair styles. To the fathers, long hair has been a symbol of slovenliness and lack of masculinity. This construct was deeply ingrained and fathers found it threatening to admit it might be in error. To the sons, long hair was a symbol of "belonging," of being accepted by their peers. To appear in the old-fashioned "skinned" look would make them feel outcasts, pariahs. Being rejected is a real threat to anyone, especially young persons who are most often fighting desperately to identify with those most admired in their age group. Many adolescents long for approval from both parents and friends. However, as with everyone, the peer group has the power to wield the strongest, most fearful weapon of rejection.

What does "Acceptance" mean? It means total acceptance of the person—of his physical self, his expressions of his individuality (dress, manner, attitudes), and of those persons, ideas, and goals with which he identifies.

Now accepting another person does not mean that you must express approval of everything he does, or that you copy his taste, or believe that he's extremely intelligent when he isn't. "Acceptance" means that you respect his "being" and his "becoming," that you avoid showing scorn, criticism, a patronizing attitude, or a judgment of any kind. Most of all, you avoid giving him advice. You see him as a fellow human being sharing the same existential dilemmas, who will, if given a chance, steadily grow toward a beautiful fulfillment of the Self.

Again I quote that source of both practical and technical wisdom, Bruno Bettelheim, who spoke to a small group of us a few years back. He was deploring the modern day parents' lack of patience and insight. He pointed out that in general parents make two gross mistakes—either they agree with every silly whim and foible of their teenage offspring, thereby reducing themselves to the same level of immaturity, or, much much worse, they argue! Dr. Bettelheim went on to reminisce about his own upbringing. His father was not trained in the behavioral sciences, but he possessed a high degree of stable, common sense which stood him in good stead as patriarch of a large family. A calm man, he sat quietly smoking his pipe as his teenagers shared with him all their rash impulses and youthful opinions. His feedback was attentive but low key, "Yah? Oh, yah? Mmmmmm. Iss dot zo!" Dr. Bettelheim went on to explain. "Now, my papa, he was no psychologist. He didn't have any fancy degrees. He hadn't read any big books on kids. But he knew human beings and he knew that, in time, we would drop our dunder-headed little boy and little girl ideas. He accepted us wherever we happened to be on our growth-ladder; and he trusted us to keep climbing."

Basically, then, acceptance means trusting that each person is, at the core, a wonderful, unique human being, endowed with value and dignity. If given a chance, he will rub off the outer shell of hang-ups and problems and become almost totally his true inner Self, that beautiful gem which needs to be dug out and polished up and put in its proper setting. But he can do all that only if you first accept him just as he is, so that he feels free to shine forth.

Such acceptance begins with acceptance of the physical appearance. If you are choosy about the color of people's skin, or if you feel everyone must have straight teeth and skinny hips, your lack of acceptance is going to stick out all over. Nor can you build much rapport with someone if you obviously resent his taste in clothes or his social customs; in short, if you demand that he conform to your standards.

The truth of the matter is that we usually demand conformity only in those we feel privileged to look down upon. When we look up to someone, truly respect him, we forgive all kinds of nonconformity. A short time ago, I attended a lecture delivered by an English woman, Freda Bedi, who many years ago married a Sikh and went to India. There she worked many years in Indian government service and then joined a high Buddhist religious order, the first Western woman to do so. Dressed in Buddhist robes, her head shaved, she was certainly a nonconformist in the eyes of the Western world. No one could deny that her clothes, her life style, her religious or political convictions could be termed anything short of "far out." But on the lecture platform, not only was she accepted, but because of her spirituality she was honored and revered. I wondered how many members of the audience were as tolerant of their own sons' and daughters' nonconforming haircuts, clothes, political attitudes, and religious persuasions.

In their desperate search for identity, young people stumble into various paths and byways of personal choices, which are extremely important to them, at least temporarily. A few calendar pages later may reveal startling reversals in such choices, but in the meanwhile it is critical for them to feel accepted, no matter which path they're traveling at the moment.

Not only does everyone crave acceptance of his self, he craves acceptance of those extensions of his self—the persons, ideas, or goals with which he identifies. The would-be "people-helper" or friend cannot create a supportive climate while sending verbal or nonverbal messages which say, "You're O.K., but what a pity you're tied up with those weird companions." Or "How can you possibly entertain such stupid ideas?" Or "Surely you're smart enough to have more ambition than that!" You may as well shoot down the person himself as to fire away at the world he's accepted as his own.

Some "generation gap" confrontations demonstrate the pain of seeing one's cherished beliefs trod upon as though worthless. In recent years the local police of a university town received a complaint from two spinster sisters in their sixties who objected to the nudity of the young men living in the fraternity house next door. Naturally, when the boys heard of the complaint, they amused themselves by deliberately parading their naked bodies in front of open windows and in their yard. The boys reasoned that the sisters could lower their shades if they didn't like the view. The outraged women, who felt that the nudity itself was immoral, not only their sight of it, grew more and more distraught. Finally the matter had to be settled by the university, but not before the staff of the psychology department and many others had become involved. It was difficult for the young men, who were really not malicious, to understand that their casual attitude toward undress was a very real and threatening personal affront to the Victorian-minded ladies, whose emotional reaction was entirely involuntary. The ladies so much identified with the moral standards of their own upbringing that such standards had become an extension of themselves, an extension which could not be amputated by changing times, reason, or any other means. An attack on these standards was an attack on them.

Most of us feel the same about religion, politics, or even less emotionally charged parts of our life style, such as our taste in food or recreation. How do you feel when you're partaking of one of your favorite exotic dishes and someone next to you says, "Ugh, how can you eat that sickening stuff! Sometimes, it seems to me you'd eat anything!" If you're like most of us, you feel a degree of put-down and rejection. At some level of your consciousness you're thinking, "He doesn't approve of my choice in food, and all my choices are an extension of me, so he doesn't approve of me."

When we truly accept another person, we respect his total living process. This does not mean we agree with all his viewpoints. It means we acknowledge that individuals have a right to controversial opinions and standards. It means we present our differing viewpoints with tact and dignity, if we present them at all. We also have enough intelligence to know exactly when it is useless to do so. It profits us nothing to attack someone's strong convictions when we know there's no possible meeting ground for such debate.

Total acceptance of a person also does not mean that we approve of outrageous or criminal behavior; it means that we recognize that such behavior is a symptom of frustration and suffering, a symptom of the need for feelings of self-worth and security. Most criminality and mental illness would be eradicated if only everyone could build self-esteem, self-acceptance, within himself. Lack of self-esteem causes fear, guilt, and anger. These demons are the perpetrators of most of the ills, physical and mental, in the whole world.

Of course, every truly skilled professional has learned to communicate his own acceptance of each patient who walks through his door, no matter what the personal history might reveal. A psychoanalyst once told me of his strangest case. A man slunk into his office, keeping his eyes focused on the floor. He said, "Doctor, it has taken me a long time to gather courage enough to come to you, but finally I knew that if I didn't do something, there would be a great tragedy. I have an awful, overwhelming compulsion. I'm afraid I can't fight it back much longer. It's certainly the worst thing you've ever heard of. I keep wanting to find a beautiful girl and strangle her to death. But that's not all of it. Then I'd take a straw, insert it into her bladder, and drink the urine!" At that point he broke down and began to cry. Between sobs he blurted out, "I'm sure you think I'm a hopeless, horrible monster." The psychoanalyst replied calmly, "No, I don't think you're a monster. I think you're a human being with a horrible problem." Fortunately the distraught man was helped, perhaps because the therapist could accept him as being basically no different from the rest of us; only his problem was unusual.

In training nonprofessionals to work on hot lines, it's been found that the most difficult lesson for them to learn is the basic rule of thumb—the more obnoxious a person's behavior, the greater his problems and the greater his need; if you're a truly dedicated "people-helper," you try to meet this need. But it's tempting to want to deal with the more pleasant people. You notice this principle everywhere, for instance in the school classroom. Everyone wants to help the loving and lovable child. But it's not the loving child who needs additional loving; it's the one who is unlovable, the one who is defiant and ugly and treacherous, likely to bite and scratch, who needs every bit of warmth and understanding and acceptance a teacher can muster. Of course, it's the same when counselors deal with adults. Both professionals and nonprofessionals enjoy dealing with clients who have only easy little problems, clients who are basically well-adjusted and secure. They respond quickly and give you a great sense of accomplishment. The really deeply troubled persons are difficult to handle, are likely to strike back or to escape into their own world of fantasy or to cling to their own inappropriate behavior.

Unfortunately, these people reinforce their low opinion of themselves over and over, often even in counseling situations which should provide the most support and encouragement. Very often their first counseling sessions go fairly well, but eventually the impatient client is disappointed with the slow progress. He then believes that his case is hopeless, that he's completely worthless, just as he suspected all along.

Sometimes we witness the miraculous effect of acceptance in its own right—how just acceptance alone can work changes in a life. I am thinking of a young man whom I'll call Larry. Larry was about twenty-two years old when he first made an appointment with me. Larry had had epileptic seizures as a preschooler and in the lower grades. Although medication eventually brought the condition under control, young Larry was soon suffering emotional damage which was to wreck his life for many years to come. His father, unbearably ashamed of his misfit son, rejected him violently and completely every day of their lives. Larry's school teachers were mystified by his behavior; his schoolmates branded him as "weird," and his teachers concurred, even though his intelligence tests invariably showed him to have average ability. He had no satisfactory companionship during his twelve years of public schooling; eventually he learned to keep to himself in order to avoid ridicule and rebuffs. In his junior year, on his daily paper route, one girl was friendly enough to smile at him each day; once she even offered him a soft drink, a kindness he never forgot. It was the highlight of his eighteen years of growing up. Upon high school graduation he attended an electronics technical school, then eventually managed to land a job. At first he was fairly happy; the other workers didn't befriend him, but neither did they jibe at him. However, soon the supervisor began to observe him closely and frequently, demanding more and more speed and efficiency. It was at this time that Larry made his first appointment with me. Not only was he emotionally unstable and feeling more and more forsaken, he was anxiously fearful of losing his job and his income. Finally, he was laid off. Then came a long period of desperate depression, months of trying to gather enough courage to look again for work. Eventually, he once more settled into a job, at first excruciatingly afraid that he would again fail to measure up, that no one would befriend him, that he would be forced to live forever in empty loneliness, without human ties of any kind. But a wonderful miracle occurred, for in this shop was a spirit of camaraderie which he never in his life before had experienced. Other workers stopped by to see whether he needed help with his assignment, girls (mostly married) flirted with him, supervisors encouraged him, everyone accepted him, shyness and all. For the first time in his twenty-three years he discovered a world glowing with kindness and friendship. And Larry blossomed. I've often wondered about that electronics company, wondered what initiated and bolstered the prevailing attitude which made an awkward, scared boy feel so surrounded by acceptance.

This kind of validation is important to build self-esteem in a person, to make him feel "O.K." The most O.K. child I ever knew was a little girl named Lisa. Lisa was neurologically handicapped and would never learn to walk or talk very well. She would never be a cheerleader, win a beauty contest, or go to college; but Lisa was O.K. She smiled a lot and liked everybody she met. She thought the world was wonderful and the world returned the compliment. All this loving interchange began with Lisa's family, who knew how to build a handicapped child's self-esteem by demonstrating total acceptance. From birth onward her parents, brothers, and sister poured out love and support to Lisa. They pampered and cherished her. She felt more wanted than do most children.

Sometimes a self-righteous paraprofessional will say to me, "Of course I accept people just as they are, but I have high moral standards and I'm not going to lower them just because I'm doing volunteer work. I intend to let people know when they're breaking laws of decency." Such a statement makes me very sad, not because I don't believe in decency, but because I know this well-meaning person is in for a lot of disappointment. What he doesn't seem to realize is that practically everybody knows about those "laws of decency" he's talking about; some people just don't choose to live by them. His moralistic preaching is not only going to be useless, it's going to turn off everyone he comes in contact with. His clients will either become hostile, or they'll just ignore him and never come back. He'll be in the same situation as the spinster sisters who objected to the college boys' nudity.

Communication will break down completely.

Other "people-helpers" believe that counseling consists in giving advice. They don't understand that they can't possibly accept a person totally and give advice all in the same breath. Giving advice carries the message, "I'm wise and superior; I know how to solve your problems. You're stupid and inferior; and you don't know how to solve your problems." The counselee is trapped, no matter how he responds to this advice-giving. If he refuses it and tries to find his own answers, he'll expect the counselor to feel insulted and to reject him. If he does accept the advice, he must make the painful admission to himself that he's childishly dependent, and the only way he can make it through life is to seek help each time he has a problem. Either way he does not feel acceptable.

Those people who are determined to give advice are most often motivated by the need to feel important. It gives them great satisfaction to feel, or even to say, later when everything has turned out well, "Look what I've done for you. Where would you have been if it hadn't been for me!" Of course this does nothing to make the troubled person feel strong and autonomous, as everyone needs to feel.

Some time ago, a newspaper subscriber criticized his psychotherapist in a letter to a lovelorn columnist. The reader complained, "Sure, I'm a lot better, but I did it all myself. The therapist didn't give me one good suggestion to follow. It makes me mad to think of the money I spent!" The columnist sympathized with the writer of the letter, agreeing that many therapists were incompetent. Her reply showed how little she knows about psychotherapy. The really skilled therapist guides his patient so gently and subtly that the patient, scarcely aware of the influence, finally learns how he himself can establish his identity and control his destiny. The therapist who attempts to solve all his patient's problems by giving overt advice is not a therapist at all.

There are other aspects of this advice-giving folly, and if you analyze them all carefully, you'll see that at the bottom of each is the principal that you cannot totally accept the person wherever he's "at" and give advice at the same time.

For one thing, usually the person you're trying to influence is not in the right emotional place to act upon the advice. As a rule, the same advice has already been given to him about twenty-five times, and if he were thinking clearly and able to follow through, he would have taken the advice a long time ago. In fact, he would probably have thought of it himself; most advice is pretty commonplace. But his emotional state prevents him from taking logical action at all.

Also, you run the risk of preventing a troubled person from making the best choice, of taking the most reasonable action, by advising him to do so. A defensive person who is filled with anger and hostility might take an exact opposite stand from the one which he was advised to take, just to show his independence. Many an unfortunate marriage would not have taken place, had not the parents advised so strongly against it.

Or you may generate a response you could not possibly foresee. Some time ago I had a client who came to me simply to develop courage enough to leave her husband. He was a sick, brutal man, and she knew she ought to have left him years before, but she had never been out in the world on her own and the prospect frightened her. I knew it would take her a while to gain the confidence she needed and was very patient with her procrastination, but her best friend couldn't see it that way at all. Each time they met, the friend would try to push her into action by attacking the husband verbally, pointing out what a beastly, odious man he was. And each time this occurred the wife felt compelled to defend her husband, the man she had once adored, which made her more irresolute about leaving him. The friend's urging almost had the exact opposite effect from what was intended!

Another disadvantage of being quick to give advice is that you might possibly never get to the real problem at all. Very often people with problems do a lot of talking and testing before they really open up about what's troubling them. They introduce other topics to see how you respond. They put out little feelers to see how you operate. For example, a boy might ask you what color shirt he ought to wear to the dance. If you're the quick-to-give-advice type, you'll immediately play all your trumps. You'll ask what color shirts he has and what color his eyes are. If he says his eyes are blue and he has one each of red, green, and blue shirts, you'll tell him to wear the blue shirt and that will be the end of that. Now the boy may not have wanted to talk about shirts at all; that may have been just for openers. But you've finished off the game before he had a chance to play another card. He may be wanting to discuss the fact that his date's father doesn't approve of him, or that he doesn't know how to tell if his date really likes him, or a dozen other questions, but you haven't given him the opportunity.

Sometimes the troubled person is a little ashamed to admit the real problem and needs to gather courage. Again, the quick advice never gives him a chance to find that courage. For example, a young boy comes home from school sobbing, "I hate my teacher!" An officious mother might admonish, "I've told you before; you've got to learn that your teacher is just doing what's good for you. Now stop being such a baby and go out and play." Or the parent might advise, "Yes, teachers these days don't amount to much. If she gives you any more trouble, you just march right down to the principal and tell him about it!" A wiser mother might say something like, "You seem pretty upset. You must feel really bad." This acceptance of his feelings would encourage the child to continue the story, perhaps of how the teacher called on him when he wasn't prepared, of how he tried to bluff it through, and how the class all laughed at his poor show. Together they could discuss the pain of humiliation and the foolishness of pretense, and how a similar situation might be handled in the future.

There are at least fourteen other reasons for not giving advice, but all you have to remember is that you can't possibly totally accept a person wherever he is at the moment and give him advice at the same time, any more than you can jump onto a horse and ride in every direction at once.

And worst of all, if you've got to give advice and to show how "right" and wise and superior you are, if you enjoy being so much in control of other people's affairs, perhaps your own level of self-esteem is not yet as high as it needs to be.

The person who wholeheartedly accepts himself feels perfectly comfortable letting other people run things, especially things like their own lives. Such a person is content to sit back and let other people grow, each at his individual pace, trusting the human spirit to find its own way, knowing that maturity cannot develop without the experience of making one's own choices, at times making one's own mistakes.

You've probably known parents who begin almost every communication with their children with such phrases as "You better do . . .," or "I *told* you to . . .," or, "You should . . .," or "Why didn't you . . .?" These bossy, controlling parents are determined to keep their offspring in the roles of helpless, immature, dependent children.

You might ask, "But what should I do when someone INSISTS he wants my advice?" As will be pointed out later under the subject of problem solving, you can help the person to be resourceful about discovering choices, and you can help him examine those choices in order to act upon the most appropriate one. This is not the same as giving advice, for you are not directing his behavior, not selecting what's best for him. He makes his own decision. Of course, if the advice concerns simply objective information, such as informing a friend what kind of wardrobe would be suitable for the tropics in the middle of summer, your answer is obviously not in the same category as advising whether she should change jobs, or marry the local tavern keeper, or stop speaking to her sister-in-law.

Perhaps the merry-go-round of acceptance and self-esteem should be more accurately described as a spiral, beginning with tiny circles and gradually broadening out wider and wider. The first acceptance of others will lead you to a measure of self-esteem. As you find the beauty and tenderness in others, you find it in yourself; as you find you can allow others to be realistically human, you find you can allow yourself the same privilege. You begin to find tolerance for the human dilemma. You see yourself and everyone else in the same lifeboat, all struggling to survive, like a crew of awkward children. Some are standing up in the boat when they should be sitting down, some are rowing the wrong way, some are getting terribly seasick, and everyone is pretty scared, but all are bumbling along the best they know how. And you're doing just about as well as anyone. Your empathy and understanding widen into greater and greater circles. Others feel the warmth of your acceptance and return it to you powerfully and the circles widen still more.

In order to understand thoroughly the constructive effect of acceptance, we ought to consider for a moment the destructive effect of its counterpart, rejection. First, what is rejection? It's any denial of a life or an aspect of a life. It points out weakness or worthlessness. If an acquaintance invites you to dinner and you refuse, preferring to watch a fatuous TV show, you obviously believe that his company is worth less than the entertainment on TV. You've rejected him. If in addition to refusing his invitation, you ridicule his choice of menu, the other friends he's invited, and his conversational skills, you've also conveyed your belief that he's a weak, ineffectual human being because you wouldn't insult him so openly if you feared any kind of retaliation. Now you've rejected him in a slightly different way from the first rejection. You've humiliated him, which probably makes him feel impotent and helpless. If he's like many people, he feels very threatened, for certain aspects of his life have been invalidated. Of course, if he has a very well integrated ego, he can shrug off your rejections, realizing they do not really make him less of a person. After all, he's the same person he was before he issued the invitation. However, such ego strength is rather rare, especially in young people.

Children who, for one reason or another, have been rejected over and over while growing up cannot build self-esteem or any sense of security, because over and over they've internalized the verdict, "You are worthless and impotent. You are not O.K." This not only weakens the ego but implants anxiety, for instinct tells them that worthless, impotent creatures do not survive.

Has it ever occurred to you that practically every negative emotion grows out of rejection or the fear of rejection? From birth to death (the final rejection) we struggle to avoid rejection, that threat to our survival. Guilt, hurt feelings, feelings of inferiority, insult, disappointment, lone-liness, jealousy, failure, disgrace, embarrassment, betrayal, disillusionment, all these and many more can be associated with rejection. Some of these feelings turn into hate and anger, the secondary emotions which we summon in order to fight back. It is said that all guilt turns into resentment. Let that be a warning to those parents who control their children by making them feel guilty and obligated. The end result is bitterness.

We should further consider that almost every human contact yields some degree of either acceptance or rejection, often communicated so subtly that each participant is almost unaware of the cause and result. The communication may be by word, tone of voice, gesture, action, or the omission of any of these. If you say hello to someone and he fails to notice you, you feel rejected, ever so slightly perhaps, but still rejected. Even if he responds, but looks puzzled so that you know he's forgotten your name, you still feel some small measure of rejection. However, if his face beams as he says, "Why hello, there, Reginald; good to see you," the meeting has rewarded you with a measure of acceptance. The more insecure a person is, the lower his self-esteem, the more sensitive he is to real or imagined rejection. He may strike back, he may simply wilt, or he may do both, in that order.

Childhood memories often evoke some hurtful feelings of rejection, for the child is usually sensitive to his helpless-ness and doubtful of his worth. Often he feels dumped, thrown overboard by the adults in his life who should demonstrate empathy and understanding, or by his peers who are concentrating on their own struggle for identity. Cruel jibes or berating from his friends are usually tempor-ary torments, but the constant criticism, correction, and ordering about that often goes on at home tatoos the tender ego day after day with the message, "You aren't worth much." Groucho Marx once coined the remark, "Home is where you hang your head."

Even as adults the slightest rejection can affect our mood. How do you feel when the boss hints that your work is not up to par? Dejected, no doubt. How do you feel when someone is too busy to talk to you? How do you feel when you bring home a bouquet of flowers and your wife doesn't bother to tell you how wonderful you are or thank you but just murmurs indifferently, "Oh, yeah. Just put them down somewhere, anywhere, and I'll try to get to them later." Or, if you are Polish, how do you really feel, deep down inside, when someone tells a "Polish joke?" The ridicule is thinly veiled by humor, a snide way to build ego at another's expense.

Some people feel the frustration of rejection if the phone is busy when they try to call, or if they are answered by a tape recording instead of a human voice. Most people resent the rejection evidenced by being interrupted. The interrupter is sending the message, "What you're saying is not important; you're not important. What I'm saying is important; I'm important." In fact our whole code of courtesy is based on avoiding any show of rejection. Instead, the kind, courteous, gentle, person emphasizes acceptance.

In a real sense, acceptance is an aiding and abetting of life and growth; rejection is a threat of annihilation, death. The early Greeks glorified the quality of courage, fully aware that courage, either moral or physical, means taking a risk of being rejected on some level of being. However brave and admirable such action might be, most people with problems are in no position to exercise extreme courage; they can't afford to risk any more rejection. Instead, they need all the acceptance they can gather, from whatever source possible.

3.

How to Be a Winner

The most vital activity of any friend or "people-helper" (employer, spouse, parent, counselor) or anyone who is interested in building good interpersonal relationships is listening—and listening and listening and listening. If you want a friend for life, listen to him. If you want a relationship for life, listen—truly listen to each other, for nothing so permanently binds two people together. It is the basis of all real love. Without it there can be no communication, no depth of understanding. It is a skill which requires intelligence and practice, but without it relationships wither and die. Listening is basically a giving of the self; its generosity is palliative.

Nothing else is as validating as listening; it is the most subliminal but powerful form of acceptance. We are verbal creatures ("In the beginning was the word"), and each statement we utter carries not only its individual, specific message, but its general message which says, "I AM." But if no one listens, if no one understands, if we are constantly interrupted or cut off, the message is echoed back, "I AM NOT."

You have probably come in contact with the two extremes of talkativeness—the compulsive talker who doesn't allow anyone else to squeeze a word in, and the person who is almost clammed up completely. Each one has had too many "I AM NOT" messages ground into his psyche. His lack of security has influenced his communication pattern. If you've ever had an experience of being lost in a foreign country and not being able to break the language barrier, you will have had a small taste of the emotions which go into the "I AM NOT" messages.

Many years ago I found myself all alone on the waterfront of a Chinese port. The small boat which had brought me ashore had left. I'd expected to be met by some business associates of my husband's, but messages had gone astray, so there I was at sunset, all hundred pounds of me, clutching my suitcase. Lined up close by were about twenty rickshaw boys, watching curiously and exchanging remarks in Mandarin, but none of them understood English. I didn't dare leave the spot. All the buildings in the vicinity were closed up tightly for the night and I had no idea what lay beyond. Besides, if I wandered around, my friends would probably never find me. The rickshaw boys finally began to crowd closer. One or two plucked at my sleeve, one pulled at my suitcase. I never remembered being so very terrified before in my whole life. As I closed my eyes and fought back the hysteria now rising in my throat, I realized that I could put down the fear if only these people could understand me. It was the lack of communication, much more than the being alone in a foreign country, which was tearing at me.[2]

The term "listening," in either a friendship or counseling situation, does not mean only keeping quiet while another person speaks. It means behaving nonverbally and verbally in a manner which promotes understanding and encourages the speaker to communicate fully and to experience the forceful "I AM" feeling.

First, let us consider nonverbal communication, especially as it relates to listening skills. Much has been written about "expressive movement," now sometimes called "body language." Some popular paperbacks (not all of them authentic) on the subject have drawn attention to the fact that particular gestures and postures usually convey particular messages.

While listening to a person, you'll want your body to say to him, "You are important. I want to hear and understand your every word." In that case, you'll be as attentive as possible, not with just your ears, but with your whole mind and body. You'll not be checking your watch, playing with the dog, popping your gum, swinging your feet, drinking a cup of coffe, or anything else which makes it look as though a part of you is concentrating on something else. Rather than lounged back in a half-reclining position, your body will look straight and alert; you'll keep eye contact most of the time. In this way you'll communicate the "you're important" message. But each time you let your eyes wander to something out of the window, doodle on a scratch pad, or brush the lint off your jacket, you are sabotaging your own communication.

In our daily lives there is constant sabotage of the "you're important" message. Have you ever had a consultation with your doctor, only to have the phone ring four or five times? As he turns his back on you each time to answer it and then ignores you for the next few minutes, you try to tell yourself that this prestigious person is much in demand and must spread his vital attentions among all the sick and dying, but nevertheless, there creeps into your mind the nagging complaint that you ought to be the most important person to him right this minute. You're the one who made the appointment and is paying for his time. You feel a certain insidious put-down.

Much the same thing happens in the home. The husband comes from work and sits down to his cool drink or snack. Before his wife can tell him about the party she's planned, or the new neighbors who've moved in, he picks up the sports section of the evening paper and begins to read. When she protests, he retorts, "Go ahead, I'm listening." He doesn't even hear the silence which follows. But Mother is just as guilty. Son comes home from school, still caught up in the excitement of the ballgame he's just won, almost single-handed. Dad is reading the paper, so Son turns to Mom. By this time she's busy preparing dinner, but she flings the "Go ahead, I'm listening" over one shoulder. He tries to compete with the slam of the refrigerator door, the banging of pots and pans, and the whistle of the teakettle, all the while dogging Mom's tracks from one end of the kitchen to the other. Finally, he gives up and goes into the other room where he phones his girlfriend and shares the play-by-play report with her. Later on the parents say, "You can't get a thing out of kids these days. They won't talk to anybody."

But if the home has its communication problems, the business world is not much better off. It's common knowledge that many of the people in executive positions flub up completely on communication and then wonder why there's so much absenteeism, why there's so little loyalty to the company, why no one seems to work any harder than he has to. Most of us have either experienced or observed a management versus employee kind of meeting now and then. The exact purpose of the meeting doesn't matter. Usually Employee is on time and has about twenty minutes in which to absorb the nonverbal message of the room itself—the impressive proportions of the room, the luxurious carpeting, the massive desk cleared of everything except an extremely expensive photo of an extremely expensive female, and the bookcase which obviously houses a built-in bar. Eventually Mr. Management charges through the door, with no apology, no explanation, no greeting. He gives only a brief nod in the general direction of Employee as he picks up the phone. He barks a few orders to let everyone know he won't stand for any nonsense, and then delays still longer while he fumbles through coat pockets, drawers, and so on. Eventually he locates a cigar, which takes an extraordinarily long time to light. Finally, he puffs and glares toward Employee with a puzzled look which says, "Now let me think, who *are* you?" During this time he is leaning far forward, both hands spread out on his large desk, elbows out, as though ready to spring. Employee mumbles his name and something about having an appointment. This brings a look of relaxed recognition to Mr. Management's face, also a change of posture. Now he leans far back in his swivel chair, gazes at the ceiling, and swings half way 'round so that Employee can see only one ear and shoulder. At long last he permits some conversation, but nothing he says can make much difference. He couldn't possibly drown out his body language, not even if he stood on his mahogany desk and shouted at the top of his lungs!

Another form of nonverbal communication is facial expression. Everyone feels more comfortable around people who smile at least part of the time. Of course, a continuous smile looks set and phony. But faces can express criticism, worry, anger, or stress. Unfortunately, some of these expressions are not always in keeping with the thoughts going on behind the face. A person's angry frown may mean only that he's concentrating, or a scowl may mean that he can't see very well. Some truly candid camera snaps would probably be a revelation to most people.

Like the facial expression, the voice doesn't always express its owner's outlook accurately, but the listener is impressed by it just the same. A rich, warm, modulated voice gives the impression of love and concern, while a strident voice jars the senses and upsets the mood of confidentiality and close rapport. Unfortunately, many conniving con men sound like song birds, whereas many loving, concerned people sound like cackling hens.

However, certain attitudes of impatience, criticism, or indifference are unmistakenly expressed by the voice, regardless of how musical or unmusical its natural quality. Have you ever been in a room with a parent, a child, and a telephone and had this fact demonstrated? Perhaps we've all heard something like the following: Mother is busy in the kitchen when Teenage Daughter enters. Without looking up, Mother mutters impatiently, "Hello. . . Oh, it's you!" Teenage Daughter quietly apologizes for interrupting, and the

Do People Really Listen?

To learn the answer to this question, read each of the following sentences, one at a time but without repeating, to a friend or member of your family. Ask him to repeat the EXACT message, word for word, of each sentence.

1. My father wanted me to be a great football player, so he wasn't very pleased when I majored in ballet and minored in mosquito abatement.

2. The bermuda grass has taken over our lawn and the bank has taken over our grand piano.

3. Some burglars got into our house last night and stole our flannel nightgowns and my uncle's wooden leg.

4. Paul Fowler was a pharmacist's mate in the navy. Now he's a topless dancer at the Purple Carrot Pinball Machine Casino.

5. Nine times out of eight I get to work on time, but today the traffic was heavy and I got mugged in Central Park.

6. I'd like to buy a pair of brown sox, woolen and nylon mixture, size 10, with heavy ribbing and reinforced toe and heel.

7. My friend, Joe Hildebrand, had a date with me for Thursday night, but he broke it to go to the Chowder and Marching Society bimonthly meeting.

8. Most of the summer TV programs are reruns which I've already seen. However, there's a new series called "Flying Low Over High Buildings" which is new and exciting.

9. The art museum in San Francisco is having an exhibit of old Chinese art; our class plans to see it this Thursday, but my sister's class won't see it until the following Tuesday.

10. The theater was hot and crowded, so I really enjoyed the double bill of "The Mad Mob from Soho," and "Another Knight Who Spent the Day Looking for a Weak Sister."

11. I wanted to buy four jingle bells with woolly clappers and purple ribbons, but the saleslady had just sold them all to a little fat old man in a red suit.

12. Once I tried to learn to play chess, and several times I tried to learn to play Kick the Can; but I think I have either a glandular disorder or a rare, exotic virus which prevents me from mastering those complicated, competitive games.

13. My Aunt Frizzly always made me feel as though I was fat, ugly, and stupid; but actually I was more popular than my sister, Jane, and smarter than my brother, Elmer.

14. I don't know why the candy man was upset when I said I wanted three butterballs, seven caramels, two butterscotch squares, and one turtle.

15. To get to Bergman's you drive south on Highway 22 for nine miles, then turn north to the covered bridge, then go down river to the falls at the fish hatchery; however, I don't think anyone is home this month.

mother's reply is heavy with irony, "Oh, that's all right! I have *plenty* of time. I'm really not doing anything. What did you want?" T.D.'s soft voice can barely be heard as she mentions going shopping. Now the mother really does let go as she blasts out, "I'm sorry! (oh no, she isn't). But I've already explained that to you! You *know* I can't go!" Teenage Daughter melts out of the room. Now the phone rings. The mother picks it up and answers in warm tones, "Hello." (She's pleased and surprised.) "Oh, it's you!" Then in her most hospitable voice, "Oh, that's all right. I have *plenty* of time. I'm really not doing anything. What did you want?" Now evidently the friend pleads with her to change her mind about an invitation. The mother answers with charming regret, "I'm sorry! But I've already explained all about that to you. You know I *can't* go." The words are exactly the same in the two conversations, but the mother's message to each is absolutely antithetical. To the daughter she implies "You're in my way. You're not wanted. You're not worth much." To the friend she implies, "You're so valuable that I always have time for you. I'm eager to keep your friendship."

Of course the exact comparison would never occur in real life, but in too many families children seldom hear a warm, affectionate voice from their parents. The tone is often impatient, sarcastic, critical, or imperative. It doesn't really matter that their parents basically love them and care about them; the children are taking a verbal beating most of the time. Day after day they're getting the message, "You aren't worth much."

Other nonverbal communication is what we now call "touching," a simple term meaning casual, low-key physical expression of friendship. This includes the handshake, pat on the back, arm across the shoulder, hugging, and so on. Cultures throughout the world vary widely in this social custom, but most animals and humans incorporate some kind of touching ritual into their acceptance of one another. In more puritanical times, we in our country did not feel so free to "touch." Boys and girls did not, for the most part, hold hands in public, and very few people embraced upon meeting. A very formal handshake was about as far as anyone dared go in public, and even in that case, a lady was to have the choice whether to proffer her hand or not. If not, the man kept his mittens to himself. When children reached a certain age, their "touching" was very carefully supervised. In fact, in some parochial schools boys and girls had to remain at least twelve inches apart and nuns were equipped with tape lines to make sure the rule was not violated.

In our present romantic revolution, when feelings have finally come into their own again, "touching" is considered natural and warm, a way of expressing our acceptance of one another. Now, ironically, we've gone almost to the other extreme, where the nontoucher is regarded with suspicion. He is looked upon as a cold fish, suspected of harboring feelings of hostility. Society has a difficult time allowing its members free choice, even in anything as trivial as this.

Another nonverbal communication is one which you may not hear mentioned much, but is important just the same. We all express ourselves by the way we dress and groom ourselves; clothing behavior is an unspoken language accepted and understood in its symbolic meaning. Again, the matter of custom and fashion has a great bearing upon our appearance, but there are many details which express attitude and individuality. The person who is overly sloppy wants to send a message of some kind. Perhaps he's saying, "Prove you love me and accept me, no matter how I look. I'm testing you." But he's more likely to be saying, "I know these aren't your kind of clothes, so my wearing them proves my independence of you and your generation," or "your social class," or whatever. At the same time, the person who over-dresses is also trying to meet some need. Perhaps he's trying to prove that he's a financial success, or that he "belongs" to a particular social stratum; or perhaps he's simply trying to attract attention. Anyone to whom clothes are inordinantly important in order to make a particular impression is trying to fulfill some emotional need.

Just one more word about nonverbal communication before getting into a different area. Perhaps the most significant aspect of nonverbal communication is your very presence. Just being there. Some of you don't have any choice. If you're a bartender or a hairdresser or a member of one of those other occupations who is invariably trapped into listening to customers' woes, you don't have to think about being conscientious and available. However, if you have an appointment with an employee who wants to air a grievance, or if you've volunteered for a "people-helping" organization, or if you've promised a troubled friend or relative he can rely on you, then you do much more harm than good if you don't follow through. Often people believe that if they're performing a service for free, they have no obligation to keep appointments or to be available as they've promised. Perhaps that would be true of many kinds of service, but when you promise an emotionally tangled person that he can depend upon you, you'd better be there, and on time. Tardiness conveys the message loud and clear, "My time is more important than yours; I'm important, you are not!"

Even if the emotional support you've promised is not for a particular problem or trouble, but just ordinary day-to-day support you give as a parent or spouse, your availability is the first requisite of such support. Over and over again in my office I listen to people who say, "I never get a chance to talk to my mother," or "My wife and I never get an opportunity to discuss things." Then I check out these unbelievable reports and I find they are absolutely true. What is even more unbelievable is that practically no one thinks this is an unusual circumstance.

The other day a married couple kept an appointment which had been made by the wife a week earlier, without consulting the husband. He was still vague about the purpose of the visit even as they both arrived in separate cars on the way home from their jobs. He was also somewhat worried; they'd been to me for marriage counseling quite some time back, but he was under the impression that everything was now going smoothly. As it turned out, the only real reason for their visit was to straighten out their vacation plans! They'd tried to make plans in snatches of conversation on the run, but in this way could not possibly come to any settlement. While in my office the wife learned that the husband invariably gets seasick on a boat and therefore hates cruises. He also suffers some airsickness on a large plane, but would be willing to endure that for a few hours. In turn, the husband learned that the wife didn't really want to go to Alaska; he hadn't realized that before. He also learned what her summer work schedule would be, when the three children would be attending summer school and what courses they had selected. For the privilege of exchanging this top secret information, they paid me my regular fee and made an appointment for the following week so that they could continue, with only a minimum of commentary from me, their rather pedestrian conversation in the quiet seclusion of my office. I was forced to conclude that their busy lives preclude any communication except that which is purposely scheduled. At home their availability score is zero.

So much for the nonverbal aspect of listening. Now what about the verbal part? Perhaps you assume there's no such thing. Listening is listening. You've been doing it for years. You just keep your ears open and try not to interrupt too much. Assuming this is the most effective method (which it isn't), most people have actually done very little listening. Have you ever sat back and observed two persons engaged in conversation? Usually it's not truly a conversation. Conversation means interaction, but most social talk is not interaction or interchange at all. It's two monologues going at once, with each person waiting to jump in just as soon as the other one takes a breath. If there are four persons in the room, someone is bound to see to it that there are four monologues going at once, even though the first ones were fairly interesting. At the end of the evening, most people cannot remember what anyone else said, unless it was something irritating or shocking; no one has listened. With everyone wanting to get into the act, most people think you're a marvelous conversationalist if you just let them do most of the talking!

A "people-helping" situation differs from a social situation in that the counselor, be he best friend, parent, or whatever, always lets the person seeking help do about ninety-five percent of the talking, the counselor using his five percent to focus and guide the session.

When Dr. Carl Rogers first developed this "client-centered counseling," he believed that most troubled persons would work out their own problems if given a chance to talk freely. About all that was required, he claimed, was a warm, accepting atmosphere which permitted the counselee to open up and reveal whatever was on his mind. The counselor was to make practically no response at all, no matter what happened. The whole burden was on the client. As I remember those early demonstration tapes, I got the impression that Dr. Rogers only grunted now and then. If the client said something really dramatic, such as, "I'm going to jump out the window," Dr. Rogers would perhaps grunt twice. Actually, he didn't grunt, he said something like "Mmmm" or "Ah-hmmm." Out in the field, most Rogerian counselors used a few more words, phrases like "Is that so?" or "Tell me about it," or "I'm listening, go ahead." Eventually we termed this technique "passive listening."

At the time Rogers developed this method, his own clientele consisted mostly of fairly emotionally healthy college students who didn't really need thoroughgoing therapy. However, other counselors with a different kind of clientele found that their more confused, troubled patients needed the counselor to take a more active role. The client still did most of the talking, but there was a subtle, therapeutic kind of feedback.

This feedback by the counselor is now called by one of several terms—"active listening" (as opposed to "passive listening"), "listening in depth," "effective listening," or "reflective listening." There are probably several other terms I've missed. I prefer the term "reflective listening," because I think that most nearly describes the method. *The main core of the system is to reflect to the speaker the gist of what he's just said.* Of course, you do this briefly so that the counselee is doing that ninety-five percent of the talking. You may think the whole idea is pointless or immaterial or ineffective or simplistic, but it is certainly none of those.

In the first place, it takes tremendous concentration. In the passive type listening, it doesn't matter if you miss a few phrases; but in active listening, you must catch every single word, else your reflecting will be faulty, betraying the fact that you don't believe the speaker is important enough to deserve your close attention. You must also be sensitive to the mood and feeling expressed; you must "think along with" the client every moment so that your paraphrase not only will reflect the facts but also will underscore the exact emotions and attitudes which the client is experiencing.

A vivid example of reflective listening technique was demonstrated in Virginia Axline's book entitled *Dibs: In Search of Self*,[3] a touching, tender documentary. Dibs was a seriously disturbed boy whom Dr. Axline treated over an extended period of time in a play therapy situation. Dibs' recovery was phenomenal. Reading the book not only would give you several hours of pleasure, but would give you great faith in the reflective listening technique. I will quote a few lines from it by way of illustration, even though the full impact can come only from reading the book itself.

Dibs, allowed tremendous freedom in the playroom each week, felt at ease to do or say whatever came to mind. His family consisted of his father, mother, sister, and himself. Most of his chatter and games centered upon stories about his family, especially his father.

If you analyze Dibs' prattle and Dr. Axline's answers, you will find that mostly the therapist does little more than mirror the statement. She repeats some of the words, or else she paraphrases the statement. Sometimes her paraphrase sums up a feeling or a situation:

> "I will punish you for everything you have ever done!" Dibs cried out. He put the father doll down in the sand and came over to me. "I used to be afraid of Papa," he said. "He used to be very mean to me." "You used to be afraid of him?" I said. "He isn't mean to me any more," Dibs said. "But I am going to punish him anyhow!" "Even though he isn't mean to you now, you still want to punish him?" I said. "Yes," Dibs answered. "I'll punish him." "He is my father," he said. "He takes care of me. But I am punishing him for all the things he used to do that made me sad and unhappy." "You're punishing him for all the things he used to do that made you so unhappy?" I said. He walked around the playroom, smiling happily. "Papa took us out to the beach Sunday in the car. We went way out on Long Island and I saw the ocean. Papa and I walked out to the edge of the water and he told me ... the differences between oceans, lakes, rivers, brooks, and

ponds. Then I started to build a sand castle and he asked if he could help me and I gave him my shovel and we took turns. We had a picnic lunch in the car." "You had a good time out with your father and mother," I commented. "Yes," Dibs said. "It was nice. A very nice trip out to the beach and back. And there were no angry words. Not any." "And no angry words," I commented.

In the first stages of counseling it is important to concentrate on feelings. Remember that the speaker must learn to recognize, define, and express his emotions, and that you are providing an accepting atmosphere so that he feels free to do so. Do not be afraid of tears or anger. All expressions of emotion are equally acceptable. Later on, after the emotions have been thoroughly ventilated, you will nudge the client toward problem solving. Each counseling case is different. Sometimes, perhaps in the case of a child whose feelings have been hurt by his teacher, his mother the counselor will concentrate on letting him ventilate his emotions for only five minutes, then she will help him solve the problem. Other times, for instance, in the case of a divorce or the death of a loved one, the listener, perhaps a friend or relative or minister, will allow the ventilating of the emotions to go on for many sessions, until the grieved person feels capable of moving forward toward some rational decisions about reconstructing his life.

In your own practice of reflective listening, whether you use it in your office, your home, at school, among friends, or in a counseling center as a paraprofessional, you will probably find that you fluctuate among the following procedures:

1. Mirroring:

In mirroring you pick out the most significant emotion expressed and feed back the exact words. Of course, if the speaker has not expressed an emotion, you cannot mirror the emotion. You will have to pick out the most significant fact which has been verbalized. Some counselors call this "parroting" and feel uncomfortable with it. However, you will find much of it in *Dibs*, and I've known many people to read the whole book without noticing that Dr. Axline did this at all. One thing about mirroring in this manner—it is safe. You

don't run the risk of mistaking or misinterpreting the
speaker. However, anyone who finds it disturbing should use
something else. The statement can be turned into a question
in order to draw the speaker on. The interrogative form also
prompts the speaker to doublecheck his own statements for
precision and sincerity.
Example:
Statement-"He's treated me like a dog, and I really hate him"
Feedback-"You really hate him?"
Statement-"Yes, I do. All the time I worked for him he made
me feel put down and worthless."
Feedback-"He made you feel worthless."
Statement-"I also feel pretty foolish that I put up with him
for so long."
Feedback-"You're feeling foolish too."

2. Paraphrasing:

Paraphrasing, which means restating in your own
words, will be used in the bulk of your active listening. If you
examine any verbal statement, you will notice that usually it
can be analyzed in three ways: the words themselves, the
emotion, and the idea. A sample sentence would break down
as follows:
"Then that so-and-so son of mine
threw a tomato, at me, his own
father!"/words ———→
Anger/emotion ———→
Son threw tomato at father/idea

As stated previously, in the earlier stages of counseling
someone you would reflect back the emotional content of the
statement, because at this point he would need to discover,
define, and accept his emotions before going on to solve his
problem or problems. You make certain you do not over-
state or understate the intensity of feelings. You're also careful to define the emotion accurately, careful not to color the
picture with your own interpretation or attitude. In order to
accept the person wherever he is at the moment, you must

remain objective, resisting the tempation to manipulate.
Later on, when the counselee can handle his emotions more
competently and is ready to attack his problem, you can begin
to reflect the idea content of his statement, in order that he
can see it more sharply and work toward problem solving. Of
course, this progress from emotion to idea is not cut and
dried. You will mostly be lead by the client himself and will
not have to worry for fear you are committing an egregious
error. As pointed out earlier, you might go through these
stages, from expression of emotion to problem solving, in
five minutes, or it might take months. In business firms a
personnel manager or a supervisor handles many "gripes"
each day, taking, in each case, anywhere from thirty minutes
to an hour. First he listens to strong feelings and then helps
solve the problem. As with the mirroring, you may turn the
paraphrase into a question in order to draw the speaker on
and encourage him to be explicit.

Example:
Statement-"He's treated me like a dog and I really hate him.
Feedback-"You despise him."
Statement-"All the time I worked for him, he'd try to make
me look stupid in front of other people. Or he'd point out
every little mistake I made."
Feedback-"He made you feel really put down?"
Statement-"Yes, but even worse, I can see that it was my
fault for putting up with the whole dumb situation for so
long. Why didn't I have more sense?"
Feedback-"You're also feeling a little foolish."

As you can see from the foregoing, some of the client's
remarks did not state an emotion, but the counselor picked
up the emotion behind the remark and expressed it.

3. Clarifying:

By clarifying, the counselor helps both himself and his
client to define feelings and situations precisely. In some instances the client has not found the exact words. In others,

the counselor has simply misunderstood. In still others, the client has generalized too broadly. Requests for clarification are never resented by the speaker. He invariably recognizes the implication: "You are important to me, so it is important that I completely understand you and everything you say."
Example:

Statement-"It was a loveless marriage from the beginning; I knew that."

Feedback-"Do you mean that you both knew that neither of you loved the other? Or do you mean that the love was just one-sided?"

******

Statement-"Everybody knew I hated my mother-in-law."

Feedback-"*Everybody* knew you hated her?"

******

Statement-"I don't know. I used to be a good Christian, but now I don't go to church. Everything is going wrong in my life. It seems that God doesn't care about me any more; maybe it's because of what I've done."

Feedback-"Are you feeling guilty about not going to church? Or are you referring to something else you feel you've done wrong?" *you are actually giving him the question to answer, but have clarified the words.*

4. *Summing Up*:

By summing up a number of rambling statements, the counselor helps the client center upon his prevailing emotion or problem.
Example:

Statement-"I lost my job and then my dog died. I really don't like where I'm living. I've tried and tried to find work but there's no opening in my field."

Feedback-"So many areas of your life seem to be falling apart. You sound pretty discouraged."

******

Statement-"My boss fired me for no reason at all. Then when I got home my wife jumped on me because our son got into trouble at school. Said I'd spoiled him. I can't see that I've ever gotten any of the good breaks in life."

Feedback-"Do you feel you're getting blamed for things that aren't your fault? Do you feel abused?"

******

Statement-"I got busted last year for using drugs, but none of my friends ever get caught. And now I read in the papers about all those crooked politicians who get by with all kinds of scullduggery. And look at all the people who drive all kinds of crazy ways on the highway, but when I go just a couple of miles over the limit I get a ticket!"

Feedback-"You're resentful because it seems that many other people get by with breaking the law, while you always get caught."

5. Refocusing:

The counselor needs to know how to refocus the interview, pulling it back from nonproductive "chit-chat." You don't want to be too directive, but you also don't want to postpone the emotional growth process and subsequent problem solving. You can usually manage to refocus the speaker on what is important. If you use a question, avoid one that can be answered by a quick yes or no.

Statement-"It was such a pretty day, I just went for a ride this morning. The flowers were all in bloom and it was lovely."

Feedback-"One time you told me that you were depressed even on sunny days. How did you feel today?"

******

Statement-"Did you see that new show on TV last night? It was really funny."

Feedback-"No, I'm sorry, I didn't. I wish I had. A little while ago you mentioned that it was really painful for you to go to visit your children last week. What bothered you most about it?"

******

Statement-". . . and then I bought the green dress."

Feedback-"It sounds beautiful. Before you talked about shopping, you touched briefly on your feelings when your mother phoned. Would you like to go into that a little more?"

Of course you won't want to be too dictatorial or forceful about directing the course of the conversation. You probably wouldn't insist that the speaker endure overlong periods of painful probing. For the most part the counselee himself will judge his own capacities for emotional involvement.

However, if you are serving as a paraprofessional in a counseling center and feel responsible for the client's progress, you will keep the counseling session trained on relevant discussion topics.

6. Silence:

Do not be afraid of silence. At times it's one of your best tools. It gives the client a chance to confront his emotions and life situation in calm, quiet surroundings, so that he can see them clearly. Let the client set the pace.

In actual practice you will intersperse the above active listening techniques with many passive listening responses, even some of Dr. Rogers' *mmm's* and *uh-uhmmmm's*. Once in a while the counselee will ask you a question or want some advice or an opinion. Or he will want to know something of your personal life. In general you will avoid any advice giving or judgment. But it helps for an easy, accepting relationship if you're honest and real and don't mind sharing bits of your own experiences and life. That is, if you can do so and still keep within five percent of the talking.

As much as I abhor the negative approach, I feel it necessary to conclude with some *don'ts*, hoping they'll save you some lumps. In another chapter you've already read a whole page on the evils of giving advice, but let me add just two more reasons for avoiding that practice. Someone once defined "positive" as being "wrong at the top of your voice." Very often you'll be absolutely certain that you can solve a person's most pressing problems in a few words and will have to grit your teeth or bite your tongue to keep from spitting out the solution. You'll tend to forget that you've heard a great distortion of the truth, or that, as with everyone, your advice *could* be bad advice. You simply can't afford such a risk for people whose lives are already snarled. Another bad thing about advice is that it hooks you into the "Yah, but . . .." game. You offer a sensational solution to a hitherto insolvable problem: "You could get acquainted at the Singles' Club by going to their party next week." Then comes the "yah but . . .." "Yah, but it's a dance, and I can't dance, so I'd feel pretty embarrassed." At this point, any progress has come to a crunching halt. The counselee has just proven that his problem is insurmountable, even you can't solve it, so he doesn't have to make any effort. Now he can relax and go home to his bottle of Scotch.

Another trap for advice givers is laid by those insecure persons who cannot bear to take responsibility for their own decisions or actions. They beg for advice so that if anything goes wrong, they can quickly shift the blame: "Look what you made me do. I took your advice about investing my money instead of spending it on things I wanted and now the stock I bought is no good," or "You told me to go to college and now I've flunked out and have no job," or "You recommended Hawaii as a vacation spot and I had a miserable time." In this way the person doesn't have to admit that he has poor judgment or lack of concentration or the inability to make friends or whatever. It's all your fault for giving him bad advice.

A few mature people really do want the benefit of your experience, training, or acumen. But usually these persons will aproach their situation with some sound problem-solving techniques and will then survey several alternative choices, assuming responsibility for their final course of action.

Inasmuch as the most important function of reflective listening is to build the speaker's Self-esteem, the most imperative "don'ts" are those associated with demonstrating your own superiority, therefore, the speaker's inferiority: advising, preaching, exhorting, criticizing, ridiculing, blaming, analyzing, judging, rejecting, warning, moralizing. You've often heard such remarks: "Of course, you knew all along that you were doing wrong, didn't you!" or "You know what you are? You're paranoid," or "If you don't stop drinking, you'll soon be a hopeless alcoholic," or "You know whose fault that was, don't you!" Every one of these is a subtle or not so subtle put-down. The speaker is in the upper position, talking down to the listener. Children hear such remarks often. The results are teenage jingle-jangles.

The other classification of "don'ts" goes to the opposite extreme: Killing with kindness, arousing self-pity. These don'ts are found in such remarks as, "You poor thing! How did you ever stand it?" or "I can feel tears in my eyes as you talk." A friend of mine who's taking a class in child guidance recently told me she didn't think much of the course. She had been advised to learn reflective listening and decided to try it when her small daughter calmly announced she had a sliver in her finger. The mother immediately went into action, "Oh, you poor, sweet darling! It must hurt terribly! Come here and let Mommie take care of it. I know how horribly painful it must be." Of course the child instantly broke into violent sobs, which led the mother to pronounce the course a failure.

Another sort of too much kindness feedback is the remark which overpraises. In the first place, most praise is judgmental. Whenever you say "That's good," you imply, "I'm sitting here judging what's right and wrong. You were lucky that time, but next time I might have to say, 'That's bad.'" Also, in a way, praise puts the praiser in a superior position, like the queen who regally rewards the knight as he kneels at her feet, head bowed. You can more safely express approval by stating your own emotion. For example, instead of telling your child that she was a very good girl to bring you the potholder she crocheted, you can say, "I like that. It makes me very happy." There's another reason that praise is poor counseling technique. It tempts the counselee to distort his statements in order to please you. It conditions him to say only that which is praiseworthy rather than pour out everything that's in his heart.

One more "don't." Many counselors are tempted to probe into problems with the question, "Why did you do it?" or "Why do you feel that way?" The truth of the matter is that most people don't know why. And such a question simply makes them feel attacked, cross-examined, and pinned to the wall like a captured butterfly. They've been so conditioned to believing that every question deserves an answer that they'll make up a wild story rather than confess, "I don't know." If you feel you absolutely must satisfy your curiosity, instead of asking "Why?" you might ask, "Did you have a reason, or was it just human blind impulse?" This offers the person a way to dodge the interrogation if he wants to do so. But remember, you must be careful about too much questioning which would destroy the constructive effects of reflective listening.

Several dynamics of behavior combine to create the power and effectiveness of reflective listening, whether it's used in the counseling situation or in other personal interaction.

To begin with, the listener's undivided and supportive attention *puts the speaker in the spotlight, thereby giving him the "I AM" feeling of importance.* He feels authoritative and influential. Many people have never had much chance to play this dominant role. Children, especially, are often ignored, interrupted, or corrected when they try to express a feeling or opinion. And many adults are too submissive to demand their turn at the spotlight; their more aggressive friends and family talk faster and louder. Also, some people make no bid for center stage because they are too insecure to risk criticism or put-down. Very often a spouse will say to me, "My wife (or husband) will never talk." In the years I've been counseling, I've NEVER ONCE found this accusation to be true. Without exception she (or he) is a veritable chatterbox in the safe atmosphere of my office! Evidently the atmosphere at home is quite different. Skillful reflective listening gives every person the chance to feel dominant.

Furthermore, the listener's nonjudgmental acceptance of the speaker's message, without rejection of any kind, *makes the speaker feel he is an intelligent, worthwhile person.* Acceptance by others helps the speaker to accept himself and further increases the feeling of "I AM" and self-esteem. Clients tell me that they're made to feel inadequate, stupid and worthless in their day-to-day situation because they seldom make a remark which isn't met with advice, correction, or something like, "Now, now, you shouldn't feel like that. Cheer up. Things will look better tomorrow," or "I think you should forget all about it; it's not that important," or "What do you mean, you feel as though no one loves you. Shame on you! That's not true. I love you." All such statements are well-meaning, but they all reject some very important part of the speaker, either his feelings or his opinions. These responses carry the message, "You and your problems are making me uncomfortable so I don't approve. If you want my approval, shape up!" By contrast, reflective listening gives the speaker his right to be. It says, "I accept you just as you are this moment. I accept you on a human-to-human level, without blame or criticism, without patronizing advice or pity, without assuming that my opinions are superior to yours and should therefore be inflicted upon you. I accept you with respect and concern. I empathize with you by climbing into your frame of reference, leaving my personal frame of reference behind me." Such skillful reflective listening validates the speaker in the most potent way possible.

In addition, reflective listening allows the speaker the freedom to verbalize all feelings so that any *painful emotions can be dissipated and vanquished*. Freed, for the most part, of the plague and confusion of pent up emotionalism, the person can go on with his life in a more organized, rational manner. Often an untrained listener will try to block off the speaker's emotional outpouring by criticizing, changing the subject, or a "count your blessings" attitude. If the speaker has gotten stuck in the same emotional spot for years, he certainly ought to be encouraged to take some positive action, but if his pain or grief is recently incurred, the blocking off of the expression of emotion serves only to increase its destructive effect. Verbalizing feelings is usually therapeutic.

Further, the speaker's verbalization and its restatement by the listener *helps to clarify the speaker's thinking in order to facilitate problem solving*. Often a person isn't certain of his choices or decisions until he puts them into words and hears them echoed back to him. This "hashing out" in a nonthreatening environment allows mental processes to mature and function efficiently. When you develop your skill as an active listener, you'll be surprised at how often a troubled person will suddenly experience a personal insight. You'll hear such comments as, "I guess the truth of the matter is that I always want to have my cake and eat it too." Or, "Now that I really look at the situation, I realize I expected too much of John." Or, "I really behaved like an eight-year-old, didn't I!" Some of these insights take minutes; some take years. But active listening allows each person to grow at his own rate, and trying to push him any faster is like trying to make a half-grown burro pull a full load; he either balks or breaks down.

Moreover, in reflective listening the listener's feedback clarifies and sharpens communication so that there are *fewer interpersonal misunderstandings.* The communication conveys the message it was meant to convey. We've all had the upsetting experience of being completely misunderstood. Not long ago a husband confided to me that he was grieved to learn that his wife had really suffered for many years over a chance remark he'd made which she had misinterpreted. It occurred when he was investing in a business which would require help from his wife, who was already very busy bringing up a large family. He was concerned about the possibility that she would become overfatigued so he commented, "I hope you don't crack up," meaning he hoped she wouldn't become overtired physically. Long afterward he learned that she'd brooded for many years over the belief that he considered her mentally unstable, an idea which had never entered his head. A few words of reflective listening when the remark was originally made would have saved years of worry.

If you've taken any courses in communication, perhaps the professor has demonstrated the difficulty of decoding or interpreting verbal messages with any degree of accuracy unless feedback is used for verification. In their textbook *The Personal Communication Process,* Winburg and Wilmot[4] illustrate this notion, using a geometric drawing instead of words. As party game or classroom demonstration you might use the figure you find on the following page (which is not Winburg and Wilmot's figure). Show one half your group the drawing, which they copy onto their own paper. Then each of these persons team up with a person *who has not seen the*

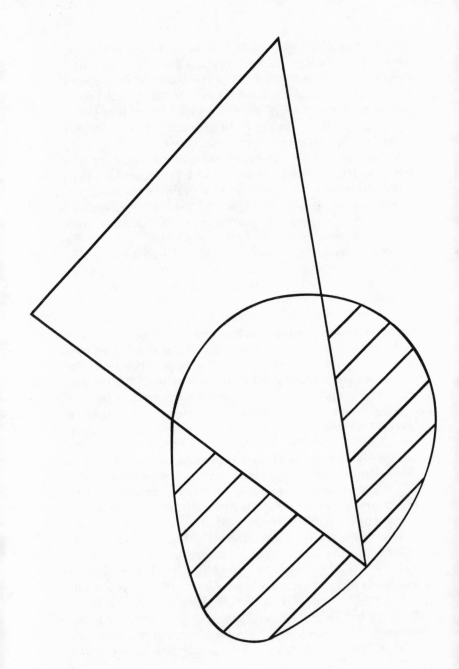

drawing, who in turn tries to reproduce the drawing by only listening to verbal instruction. No questions which might clarify the instructions are permitted, nor is the speaker allowed to watch the drawing effort in order to make corrections or add instructions. If you try this demonstration, you will be amused and appalled at the results. The drawing by each team is invariably a ridiculous distortion of the original. From these demonstrations you will learn that most verbal communication usually turns out to be stillborn. The observation explains innumerable misconceptions. When there is no feedback, no way of correcting decoding errors, communication fails hopelessly. Reflective listening, with its continual restatement and verification helps to avert gross misunderstandings.

And finally, with the use of reflective listening, the listener's attitude of acceptance along with the clear understanding between speaker and listener *create a sensitive bond, the basis of firm friendship.* Furthermore, if two persons can flexibly interchange these roles of speaker and listener, the relationship is even more rare and wonderful. The best marriages, the most successful business partnerships, and the deepest, steadiest friendships are all founded upon this exchange of openness and respect.

Everyone knows that lack of communication destroys interpersonal trust and confidence, but often no one knows how to go about establishing the verbal interaction. Many people know nothing of the skill of listening; they've never been taught. This lack of listening aptitude tends to inhibit most free expression; there's widespread fear of being misunderstood. Silence is deemed safe; but hidden feelings are far from safe. Nevertheless, they will probably remain hidden unless there is an environment of security and acceptance.

Dr. Carl Rogers himself sums it up,

> . . . as (the client) finds someone else listening acceptably to his feelings, he little by little becomes able to listen to himself. . . . While he is learning to listen to himself he also becomes more acceptant of himself. As he expresses more and more of the hidden aspects of

himself, he finds the therapist showing a consistent and unconditional positive regard for him and his feelings. Slowly he moves toward taking the same attitude toward himself, accepting himself as he is, respecting and caring for himself as a person, being responsible for himself as he is, and therefore ready to move forward in the process of being free. . . . He finds it possible to move out from behind the facade he has used, to drop his defensive behaviors, and more openly be what he truly is . . . he finds that he is at last free to change and grow and move in the directions natural to the human organism . . . he tends to move in the socially constructive direction.[5]

Reviewing these dynamics, you'll understand how the miracle of competent reflective listening fosters self-esteem, confidence, maturity, harmony, and human understanding. It should be mastered and practiced at every age, in every phase of life.

For instance, you'll find reflective listening to be one of your most valuable social assets. If you learn to use it skillfully, you will establish a deeper relationship with people. You can use it casually in ordinary conversation and then bask in your reputation as a wonderful conversationalist. Everyone loves the perfect listener. More important, you can bring it into play in any social gathering where the feelings begin to run high, as sometimes happens even in the most harmonious groups. Instead of arguing "facts" on a "He did," "No, he didn't" level, you can fall back on your listening skills and let the upset person have his say. Encourage him to do 95 percent of the talking; let him express his emotions, then paraphrase some of his statements; accept him as you would a counselee, so that his heated emotions cool and he feels comfortable.

Remember, not all your feedback will be used for the negative emotions; parents, friends, and relatives should do a great deal of just validative reflective listening day in and day out and now that you know its magical powers, you won't wait until people are in serious emotional difficulties before practicing it.

Statement-"The coach asked me to go in the last minute, and sure enough, I shot a goal that won the game!"
Feedback-"That must have made you feel wonderful."

******

Statement-"It was a beautiful day at the beach. I ran along the water's edge and jumped around and splashed, just like a little kid."
Feedback-"It's great to be so free and spontaneous, isn't it!"
******

Statement-"I want to buy Jennifer everything beautiful I see. I think of her all the time."
Feedback-"You must love her very much."
******

Statement-"Every day I wake up eager to get to the job. It's never dull."
Feedback-"You sound very happy with your job. Your work is evidently very interesting and rewarding."
******

Statement-"I was in a hurry to catch my bus, but at the post office I had to stand in line twenty minutes."
Feedback-"How maddening!"
******

Statement-"That good looking boy in my math class wants me to go out with him."
Feedback-"Are you pretty thrilled about that?"
******

Statement-"Oops! I almost dropped the goldfish bowl."
Feedback-"Gee. That's kind of scary."

Naturally, when the speaker is in a pretty good place emotionally, you don't have to be so careful to focus on the emotions, although that is the most powerful kind of reflective listening. But there are many cases where the content is very unemotional and to try to force an emotion onto it would be unnecessary, if not ridiculous. In this situation the good listener simply feeds back the main idea.

Statement-"We got up at 5:00 a.m., drove to San Francisco in an hour and then on to Sonoma in forty-five minutes."
Feedback-"You made awfully good time, didn't you!"
******

Statement-"My brother is six foot four, and my sister is five

foot nine. I have a cousin, he plays on a basketball team, who's six foot six."
Feedback-"Gee, you come from a pretty tall family."

******

Statement-"We planted daffodils over here, and marigolds over here, and chrysanthemums over there."
Feedback-"How nice. You'll have blooms all year 'round, won't you."

Perhaps you are wondering, "If I want to be considered loving and kind, am I doomed to go through life playing the role of Mr. Feedback forever? Am I never to express an opinion or state a fact again in my whole life?" On the contrary. Friendship means sharing, so you take your turn, but you make sure to deliver the feedback stroke before you grab the spotlight:

Statement-"We planted daffodils over here, and marigolds over there, and chrysanthemums over there."
Feedback-"How nice. You'll have blooms all year 'round, won't you."

and

Your Turn-"I tried to grow chrysanthemums last year. A complete fizzle! All sprawly and spindly—and the bugs really took over. But now, my roses. They were out of this world!"

Some readers will be prompted to protest, "But how can I ever win arguments if I have to use reflective listening! How can I convince my dad (or my son or my daughter or whomever) that I'm right and he's wrong if I have to stick to the rules of reflective listening, being careful never to impose my opinions?" The answer is, you can't. With or without reflective listening you can never win arguments. Invariably, arguments are a clash of emotions or head trips which have very little to do with who's right and who's wrong or a proof of either one. All they accomplish is to drive big wedges between people who then don't want to have anything to do with each other. Besides, the person who must try to prove that he's right and another person is wrong is probably a Sick Tiger type and would do well to engage in a bit of introspection to learn why he's so bent on controlling other people's lives and thinking. Why can't he allow other persons to reach their own conclusions?

This does not mean you can never compare diverse opinions and feelings. A variety of viewpoints gives the world spice and excitement and any mature person can disagree without becoming disagreeable. He does so by first listening actively to the other person and then presenting his own views without overbearing personal put-down or over-emotionalism. Good friends, relatives and even spouses are never going to see everything exactly the same way and they must accept that fact if they are to live in harmony. In some instances they may be able to compromise. Other times they may agree that they don't agree, each respecting the other's right to his own viewpoint. The important thing is that they listen to one another and cherish the relationships.

I've heard people plead, "But it sounds so *difficult!* Granted, professional counselors are skillful, because they've practiced for years and years, but I don't think I could ever learn." In truth, reflective listening is much easier than ordinary give-and-take conversation. In ordinary conversation you have to be always planning ahead about what you're going to say. Usually you try to be very clever or very entertaining or very witty; this takes a great deal of thought and ingenuity. In reflective listening you can just forget all about yourself; leave yourself out of it entirely and step into the speaker's frame of reference. In other words, BLOT OUT YOUR OWN OPINIONS AND IDEAS AND "THINK ALONG WITH" THE SPEAKER. It's as simple as that. You don't have to think; the speaker is doing it for you. If the speaker cries, "Ouch, I bumped my elbow," you mentally experience his "ouch" and say, "That really hurts, doesn't it!" If the speaker says, "Ooh, that hot soup tasted so good. I was really cold," you imagine his chilled body being relieved by the warm food and answer, "There's nothing like a bowl of good hot soup on a cold day, is there?" If the speaker moans, "I'm disgusted that Felix Higgenbaum got elected," you invite a fuller expression of feelings by reflecting, "You sound really upset." You DON'T say, "Well! *I* happen to know that

Felix Higgenbaum is much more capable and qualified, and probably even more honest, than his opponent." Oh, of course you can say that if you want to, but you're only proving that you don't believe the other person is worth much. You don't want to listen to him.

One reason that certain people resist becoming skillful listeners is that they really don't want to be emotionally involved in any unpleasantness; they don't want their own mood disturbed by someone else's distress signals. Their attitude says, "Look at me! Although I've suffered more than you have, I'm courageous and uncomplaining. Why can't you be the same?

They're convinced that if they can just talk the dispirited person out of his emotional state, the world, especially their own private world, will be a happier place. So when a child sobs, "Timmie doesn't like me any more; he was mean to me," the response is likely to be, "Oh, come now, you're just imagining things. Timmie loves you! Here, have a cookie and look at this book with all the funny pictures." Or if an adult friend confides, "I'm so frightened, I think I'm going to lose my job," the answer may be, "Oh yes, I've had that feeling at times, but you just can't let all those silly fears get you down. Cheer up and think of something else."

Unfortunately, these responses usually reap the results the listener is looking for. The speakers smother further communication and paste artificial smiles on their faces. Not because they really feel more cheerful, but because they quickly learn that only plastic, cheery masks are acceptable. All negative feelings must be jammed deep down inside where they won't show and spoil the scenes of the playacting which frequently passes for friendship or love.

Admitted, no one enjoys the companionship of constant complainers, but everyone has occasional frustrations or disappointments, large or small, and should feel free to express them to a friend or relative.

Even devoted parents often won't listen reflectively for fear they might reinforce improper behavior; they are afraid that patient listening will imply their approval of some idea or conduct that ought not be allowed. Such a theory is unsound. Listening to a child helps him to build a well integrated ego, which in turn leads to maturity and high-mindedness. True, sometimes children, in their emotional impetuosity, express themselves too strongly or not very tactfully, but so do adults on occasion. When a child blusters, "I could just kill that coach!" he probably means only that his disappointment is so great and his feelings are so explosive that he doesn't know how to handle them. If an insensitive parent pounces on him with, "Here, now young man! You march right to your room and stay there until you can show proper respect for your elders," the child's outrage is even more overwhelming. Justifiably he feels betrayed and misunderstood. If, instead, the parent says, "Gee, you're feeling pretty upset about something. Sounds as though you've had a bad time," the child will probably begin to ventilate his anger verbally and eventually, with further encouragement, will see the situation in a less gloomy light. He'll no doubt later admit he doesn't really intend to murder the coach—and he'll certainly feel that his home is a pretty comforting, supportive place. Further, the parent will find that manners and respect can be taught more effectively when moods are quieted and more conducive to rational discussion.

In my private practice I often have occasion to set about teaching reflective listening, as I find faulty communication to be the most insistent enemy of harmonious interpersonal relationships. I explain the principles, point out the need for practice, then send the person or persons on their way. Usually I begin the following session with the query, "Well, how did you get along with your practice of reflective listening?" Often the answer comes, "Oh, I didn't have a chance. I didn't have a serious discussion with anyone." Or perhaps, "There didn't seem to be any real problems coming up; I mostly just talked with friends."

The truth is that there's opportunity to practice this skill just about every time you open your mouth. And it's just as important to use it while talking casually with friends as to resort to it during an argument, perhaps more important. It builds the kind of friendships everyone needs. It rewards both the giver and receiver. If you put skilled reflective listening into practice in all segments of your life, you will discover a whole new dimension of humanity; you will understand people as you've never understood them before. There will be an interchange of love which you've probably longed for all you life.

I feel that the concept of reflective listening is so important that I never failed, during the years I was teaching social psychology courses, to bring it into the classroom. And there've been various kinds of reactions. I once presented it to a group of young parents. One father had been particularly hostile to almost every principle I'd presented, so I wasn't surprised when he declared, "Now that's the most stupid idea yet! Who on earth would want to learn to do that? It would only antagonize everybody, make 'em mad to hear everything thrown back at them! Make me mad too; I'd hate it!" I answered "You wouldn't like that, eh?" He shot back, "That's right! I'd think the person listening to me was a bloomin' idiot!" I went on, "It would just seem dumb to you." He answered more calmly, "And rude too. And not natural, just all stiff and like a game." I replied, "You'd prefer a more easygoing, casual interaction."

Not surprisingly, this man often demonstrated to us that he wasn't really interested in learning effective communication; he was interested only in proving his own power and importance. He attempted to dominate every discussion. And he admitted he enjoyed keeping his teenage children under his complete control, like well trained horses and dogs. Luckily, wiser parents in the class were eager to build rapport with their children and to help them to develop emotional security and maturity. Such parents quickly found that active listening was an important means of reaching these goals.

They also found that the general practice of active listening won personal reward. As one mother expressed it, "I'm so amazed! I used to feel so ignored, so left out; but now it seems I suddenly have more friends than I know what to do with!"

If you are afraid that reflective listening is an artificial, contrived technique, you must remember that *every* behavior, aside from basic instincts, is learned. We learn the rituals of saying hello, goodbye, thank you, and so on. We learn to share and to care for the sick and to obey the laws. We learn to bring out the best in mankind in order to develop spiritually. Reflective listening is a part of this concern for our fellowman which increases love and understanding.

Reflective Listening Exercises

Below are some hypothetical statements followed by a choice of feedback responses. Select the best response, then decide why the others are less acceptable.

******

Statement: I really feel lonely and bored today.
1. You feel you have no one who cares?
2. No one should feel bored in this exciting world!
3. Why don't you go for a walk? It's a beautiful day!
4. It's terrible to feel lonely. You feel that no one cares and that all your friends have forsaken you. Did you see that movie called "Isolation"? Dee Jones played the part of a girl who was so lonely and betrayed by her family that she tried to kill herself.

******

Statement: What a bum day I'm having! I woke up feeling really in the mood for sex, but my husband wouldn't have anything to do with me, no matter how I tried to interest him. He's so often like that.
1. Women should let men make the advances.
2. You should get your mind on something else. Bake a cake or something.
3. You must be feeling very rejected at this point.
4. You poor thing! Men can really be beasts at times.

******

Statement: I have such ugly legs, no boy would look at me.
1. Oh, come, now. Your legs can't be that bad. You're probably a little paranoid.
2. If a boy likes you only because you have beautiful legs, he can't be worth much!

3. You know that beauty is only skin deep!
4. You feel that boys are attracted by only physically beautiful girls.

******

Statement: My dad bosses me around as though I were only five years old, even though I'm fifteen.

1. You feel very put-down when your father talks to you like that?
2. You probably sometimes act only five years old.
3. Don't pay any attention. All dads do that to some extent.
4. You're probably just too sensitive.

******

Statement: I haven't had a job since high school. I just hate the idea of that old "nine-to-five" routine.

1. Everyone has to earn his way in the world.
2. Obviously, you need to find the kind of work you really like, then you won't mind doing it all day.
3. I know exactly what you mean. It's horrible to think of a whole lifetime of just work, work, work.
4. Do you feel that you couldn't adjust to doing the same thing every day? Or do those hours seem too long, no matter how much you like the work?

******

Statement: I don't want to have an abortion, yet I don't want to bring up a child by myself.

1. You feel frustrated because you can't think of a satisfactory solution.
2. Everybody has abortions these days; think nothing of it.
3. I hope you've learned your lesson so you won't get into this kind of a mess again.
4. You know whose fault this is, don't you!

******

Statement: I don't see anything wrong with a living together arrangement. What do you think?

1. You don't see anything wrong in an L.T.A., yet you'd like to know what other people think about it.
2. How do I know? I've never tried it.
3. We're not here to discuss my personal life.

4. Anyone who does such a thing obviously has a low moral standard.

******

Statement: I'd like to finish my college education, but I can't.
1. You seem to be getting along all right without it.
2. Oh, but you must. Everyone needs one these days.
3. You really have my sympathy. It's so terrible to compete with people who are much better educated.
4. You can't go back because you can't afford it, or are there other reasons?

******

Statement: I'll have to either get a divorce or kill myself.
1. Your husband sounds like a real loser. I wouldn't blame you for getting a divorce.
2. You feel you have no other choices?
3. You certainly expect a lot from a husband. You've done nothing but criticize him.
4. I know a good attorney you could see. You'd probably like to get this settled right away.

******

Statement: My father hates my boyfriend for absolutely no reason at all.
1. For absolutely no reason at all?
2. Your father probably has a good reason for this opinion. After all, he loves you and wants the best for you.
3. Some fathers are just jealous of any boy their daughter goes out with.
4. Why don't you have your mother talk it over with your father? She can probably persuade him to be more reasonable.

******

Read each of the following statements and think of an appropriate "reflective listening" response.
1. "Sometimes I hate everyone in the whole world."
2. "Praying is no good. I've prayed and prayed and never gotten what I wanted."
3. "Everybody is just out to get as much as he can for himself."

4. "I used to go to church, but I don't any more."
5. "I don't have anything to say. I just called up because I'm bored."
6. "There must be something wrong with me; I can never get a date."
7. "I had a rotten day. I was mad most of the time."
8. "I get infuriated when my kids won't help around the house. What do they think I am, their housekeeper?"
9. "Sometimes I get so depressed I don't care if I live or not."
10. "My son is in jail for drug possession and armed robbery. I don't know where to turn."
11. "I've been to counselors before. They never help anybody."
12. "Please tell me whether I should go to the police and give myself up or not."
13. "Can you help me find a good lawyer?"
14. "My wife thinks I'm made of money. She never cares how hard I have to work to keep the bills paid."
15. "I've messed up my whole life and now it's too late to start over."

4.

Problem Solving

People have problems. They made a bad investment in the stockmarket, or a storm blew the roof off their house, or the neighbor's dog killed their cat, or their daughter ran away with a bullfighter. In general, the ability to accept such problems as a part of life and then set about solving them in a practical manner depends upon the ego strength of the individual.

Very often emotionally insecure persons fall into a Hamlet routine, a wavering inability to move toward problem solving. They procrastinate, evade, make excuses, pull back—anything to avoid accepting responsibility and making a firm unretractable decision.

They are extremely reluctant to make changes in or for themselves. They mostly want a fairy godmother to wave a

61

wand and alter the environment to accommodate their own behavior. The alcoholic would like to drink without getting more than a little drunk. The overeater would like to eat and not gain weight. The critical, gossipy type would like the satisfaction of cutting people down to size without losing his friends or his job. The bossy, Napoleon type would like for people to jump when he gives the command, but not grow resentful about doing so. The dependent, overly sensitive person would like someone else to handle the bossy type for him.

In each of these situations, which often reach a desperate crisis stage, the person himself has caused the problem, yet he cannot bear to alter his behavior, which has become built into his defense mechanism. He's like a tenant clinging to the third story ledge of a burning apartment house. He'll hang on until he's burned to death or the building crashes down around around him, rather than jump to the safety net below. His reason points out the net, but his emotions hang onto the ledge. W.H. Auden expressed this resistance to change in his *Age of Anxiety*.*

> We'd rather be ruined than changed.
> We'd rather die in our dread
> Than climb the cross of the moment
> and see our illusions die.

This aversion to altering one's own behavior or taking responsibility for a situation is especially noticeable in marriage counseling. Seldom does a husband or wife say, "How can I change in order to save our marriage?" Usually one or the other opens the interview by dropping bomb after bomb of blaming. "He tries to control us all; he's a regular dictator. He comes home and criticizes each of the kids and then hides behind the newspaper. He really has never made enough money." Then comes the antiaircraft fire: "She's a lousy housekeeper. She's so overemotional, always in tears and I never know why. She spends half her time on the phone." To solve these problems will require insight, growth, and change.

---

*From *The Collected Longer Poems*, by W. H. Auden. Copyright ©1975 Random House, Inc.

Most people can modify behavior patterns to a certain extent, but basic personality structure often persists for a lifetime. Therefore counseling and problem solving which don't demand drastic transformations are the most successful.

Not only do people resist change, consciously or unconsciously, most of those who are emotionally involved in a situation simply cannot see themselves or the problem realistically. A certain old joke illustrates this point: Mrs. Bloom and Mrs. Schultz met while shopping. Mrs. Schultz exclaimed, "Why, Mrs. Bloom, how nice to see you! We haven't met for such a long time, in fact not since the marriages of your son and daughter. How are they getting along?" Mrs. Bloom hesitated. "Well, good and not so good. My son's wife, I admit I myself would not have picked. I have to face it, she's lazy. She doesn't get up to prepare my son's breakfast and doesn't even do her own housework. What's more, every penny she gets she puts onto her back. And such a baby! Every Friday night it's off to her mama's house for the whole evening! But now my daughter, she did much better. Her husband is a fine man, so understanding. Every morning he serves her breakfast in bed, even hires a housekeeper so she won't spoil those pretty hands. And so generous! Credit cards for everywhere so she can dress like the queen that she is. Besides, the dear boy brings my daughter to our home for dinner every Sunday so the family can be together all day long!"

Mrs. Bloom was not purposely distorting her story, she simply could not see her biases, so it would be impossible for her to solve any problem involving them.

Some people cannot even see how they look, how they act, and what impression they make despite bright lights and full-length mirrors. You have no doubt witnessed many examples, not only in your "people-helping," but in everyday life. For instance, you have seen the young girl who suddenly identifies with a particularly "sexy" movie star. The girl lathers herself with lurid makeup, dons ultrafreakish clothes, and adopts what she believes to be a sultry, seductive expression and irresistible wriggle. The total effect evokes both laughter and pity. Her self-image is much different from the inexperienced, awkward child she really is.

Not only children, but persons of all ages, whether troubled or not, have difficulty knowing their own minds and emotions. They give lip service to one opinion, but in actual practice they behave in quite a different way. Anyone who doesn't understand this paradox may be forced to learn a painful lesson. Some years ago a car manufacturer, puzzled about what changes to make in a new model, decided to ask the prospective customers themselves what they wanted in a new car. High speed? Plushy comfort? Flashy styling? Answers on the unsigned questionnaires indicated that the large majority of the public favored practicality, preferring durable frames and bodies, room for storage, and conservative colors rather than novel design, luxurious furnishings, or innovative "gadgets." The company, smugly overjoyed with their foolproof plans, produced the model exactly as specified. But one little thing ruined the profit and loss statement at the end of the season—almost no one had bought that car. The company skirted close to bankruptcy. To regain their previous financial stability took years and years of marketing the impratical, showy cars which the public had denied wanting.

Not only are most people unable to predict their own behavior, but they are completely unaware of their own personal "act," that unconscious role they constantly play which often gets in the way of problem solving. People cling to their "act" because of some secondary gain; it reaps attention or pity or admiration, or it helps them escape from reality, or it gives them an excuse to give up and thereby avoid risking failure. Most people would deny that they have such an "act," but a list of them (and you can add many more as you observe them) will remind you of certain persons in your life—if not of yourself.

Wearing a halo
Finding a scapegoat
Fearing the worst
Living in the past

Being brave
Chasing rainbows
Feeling abused
Waiting for the perfect situation
Threatening to shoot myself
Playing Lady Bountiful
Trying to decide
Sneering at winners
Waiting for my ship to come in
Being the "Big Shot"
Running around in circles
Barking loudly
Explaining myself
Wanting the good life, but feeling I don't deserve it
Playing ostrich

Very often the "act," deeply imbedded in the personality structure over a period of years, prevents a person from solving his problems and getting what he wants out of life. But he cannot bear to sacrifice the secondary gain it wins for him.

Many "wearing a halo" people claim they no longer want to be manipulated into spending time, money, or effort in ways which are tiresome and unpleasant. They angrily threaten to push the grown children out of the nest, or to tell the demanding, complaining widowed mother to refashion her own life, or to inform the exploitive neighbor there will be no more free babysitting. But they can't give up their "act" which they, at some level, feel identifies them as angelic "good guys." In truth the poor things are insecure "patsies" and their growing, unloving bitterness is often very apparent. The "finding a scapegoat" act allows people to avoid taking responsibility and risking failure in solving a problem. "Running around in circles" gives people the illusion they are accomplishing something whereas they're only engaging in a life of meaningless activity, which allows them to avoid the pain of meeting any problems straight on. And so on.

Keeping in mind that most human beings, especially emotionally troubled ones, do not operate in a consistent, realistic, rational manner and are often resistant to change, will keep you from expecting too much of a person you are trying to help, especially if the person is you.

In general, you will have to allow the problem solving to come from within, according to however much the person has managed to grow. One must be given the privilege of making his own mistakes, of finding his own way. Parents especially find it excruciatingly painful to stand by and allow their offspring to make blunders. Almost invariably they step in and grab the situation out of the young person's control, thereby depriving him of any opportunity to gain the experience and skill of directing his own life. Everyone learns by doing. There's practically no other way.

This does not mean that the parent or "people-helper" has no part in the problem solving. He serves mainly as a gadfly. Instead of allowing the counselee to complain forever about his loneliness, or his lack of education, or his inability to get along with his mother, the counselor prompts, "What are you doing about it?" And he doesn't accept excuses or evasions, such as "I can't help it." Gently he suggests, "Can't, or won't?" and then insists on some working toward a goal. This is not the same as solving the problem for the counselee. The counselor doesn't feed any answers or advice. He may act as a sounding board, he may try to make the counselee search out a broader spectrum of choices, or he may question violent or unrealistic choices by a subtle, "Are you certain that's what you want to do? What would be the result?" But then (except in extremely rare instances involving real disaster), the final choice is up to the counselee.

Whether you yourself have a problem or as a "people-helper" you are called upon to help someone else solve a problem, it's most effectual to use a methodical, systematic approach. The method could be seen as a number of steps leading to ultimate solution. Of course, types of problems differ widely, but the step approach can be applied to most of them.

Step No. 1. As thoroughly as it's practical or possible, let the troubled person rid himself of overriding emotion which gets in the way of seeing himself and the situation clearly.

This may take minutes or it may take weeks, but it's necessary so that reason and good judgment can prevail. A widow still overcome by the recent loss of her spouse is probably not capable of solving the problems of how to dispose of personal possessions or real estate, how to alter her life style, or how to resume her social life. When the sharp edge of grief has been dulled, which may take weeks or months, she can then be expected to make reasonable choices. In another example, an employee who's been angered by some frustration or mishap cannot be expected to discuss the matter rationally until his employer or supervisor encourages him to let off emotional steam for ten or fifteen minutes. Then the problem could receive consideration, whether it's the need for more personnel, or new equipment, or higher salaries, or more efficient organization. If the employer is wise enough to first listen actively while the employee ventilates the strong, pent-up emotion, he'll find that employee demands are made more reasonably and compromises are more readily accepted. And the person with the grievance also feels better about the relationship and about his own good, coolheaded judgment.

Fathers and mothers find that listening to this release of emotion is one of the most important functions of their parent role, listening reflectively without jumping in with criticism or advice, allowing the child to learn to select his own choices with only the most subtle nudging as to how to find these choices.

The ability to get through the emotional venting stage in a reasonable time and then down to a sound, logical solution to the problem and then carry through on that solution depends greatly upon the ego strength of the individual. Those who are immature and insecure will take longer to accomplish the full task.

Step No. 2. List the true goal or goals. This list could also be termed "needs," or "objectives."[6] If a person needs success, his goal or objective is to succeed. For the sake of consistency, these needs and objectives will be referred to as goals. The problem solver should be very specific. If he says he wants to make money, how much? If he wants to travel, where? He should also list any goal related to the problem, so that he won't solve one problem only to find he has engendered another. He might need to feel liked, but he might need just as much to design a practical budget so that he won't squander all his income on his friends.

This list will be divided into two parts: Long-range Goals and Short-range Goals. The short-range goals concern the here and now. They might include finding a new apartment, or planting a garden, or teaching a Sunday school lesson. Long-range goals cover years, perhaps a lifetime. They might include building self-esteem, or raising a family, or building a business. Long-range goals are the more important and pervasive.

Later on, as you practice your problem-solving skills, you will want the counselee to be aware of whether he's considering long-range or short-range goals; often both will be involved. However, if a twelve-year-old boy is trying to solve the problem of how to spread his weekly allowance to cover his needs, he won't sit down and list all his long-range objectives in life. He'll make a list of what he wants, like bubble gum and frisbees, and decide upon the priorities among them. On the other hand, if that boy's father comes to you, trying to decide whether or not to have an affair, he'd find it very useful to examine closely his life's goals, both long-range and short-range!

Sometimes the importance of considering the long-range goal is not readily apparent. For example, a boy might be trying to decide whether to take his new girlfriend to a high-priced gourmet restaurant or to a hamburger stand for dinner. This seems like a pretty immediate problem, one concerning only short-range goals. However, if the boy's long-range goals include paying for his own education and the gourmet dinner would cut into his budget for next semester's tuition, he's wise to take all his objectives into consideration. One source of failure for many people is that very often they aren't mature enough to keep the long-range goals in mind. They can't resist the immediate gratification of the need for pleasure.

The sad truth is that most people don't know what they

want, at least on a conscious level they don't. Ask anyone what he wants and you'll get all kinds of vague answers like, "happiness," or "money," or "a good life." None of these is a definite answer. If a genie were right on the spot, he wouldn't know what on earth to conjure up. What is "happiness?" To me it's something found only in a rinky-dink cartoon, in some simple-minded comic personality. Not that a person ought to want only concrete goals, like a villa on the Riviera; but instead of a vacuous "happiness," a thinking person might answer that he wanted life to contain significance and meaning; or he might answer that he wanted to establish his own authenticity. In counseling young people I've often asked what kind of job they wanted, and many of them have answered "anything." Now that's a very difficult job to train for! But when I'd try to get a more definite answer, their thinking would bog down completely. Many people, both young and not so young, just go along letting themselves be pulled here and there by accident or by their impulses of the moment.

If a person doesn't consciously set goals, his emotional self, sometimes an unhappy, bruised emotional self, takes over, and then he gets exactly what he wants out of life on this level. Some people argue this principle, that people get what they want out of life. One man pointed out a friend of his who'd taken care of sick relatives, one after the other, over the years. He claimed that this woman, who was married to a good, kind, successful husband, had wanted to travel and had wanted all kinds of interesting hobbies and so on, but had never been able to have much because she was constantly tied down taking care of invalids. It seems obvious that this woman got exactly what she wanted—a lot of praise and appreciation for her martyrdom!

I also argue with friends about another person, who seems to me to have precisely what he wants. My friends feel sorry for this person because he's never managed to find the "right girl." He's charming, handsome, well-educated, and well-to-do. My friends deplore the fact that girls seem to lose interest after he dates them once or twice. Actually, he doesn't date many girls; he can't get his nose out of the *Wall*

Street Journal long enough. On sunny days, instead of going to the beach, he spends his free time scouting around for available investment property. His small talk mostly concerns prime rate of interest, not a very romantic topic. But this man has exactly what he wants—money.

One woman once pleaded, "You're wrong! I most certainly do not want my mother coming to my house every week, mostly just to tell me, a forty-year-old, that I'm childish and immature." I could only answer, "Evidently you do want that, or you'd lock your door and not let her in. You're proving that she's absolutely right." Such examples of disappointment and frustration emphasize the need for setting appropriate goals so that people can work toward them for a better life.

Someone is bound to ask why it's important to let the cold, rational self have the upper hand. Haven't I already said somewhere that the loving, creative, spontaneous child within us, the emotional self, is important? In that case, what's wrong with just letting the counselor patch up the emotional self and encourage it to take over and run things. Haven't we had too much head-tripping in our culture already? Yes, I agree, the emotional self is important too; we would be feelingless robots without it. Carl Jung said there ought to be a fine balance between the two, the mental and emotional, and some people are lucky enough to have this, without any counseling. However, these are not the ones who need "people-helpers," at least not very often. The ones who need "people-helpers" are most often the ones whose emotional selves are pretty hurt and mixed up. They're like the emotional self of the woman who sacrificed her whole life to take care of sick relatives so people would love her, or the young man who'll never have a wife and family because he can't interrupt his drive to acquire security in the form of money, or the forty-year-old woman who can't give up clinging to her mother. These kinds of persons need humanistic counseling so they can handle their emotions, but they also need to establish logical, practical goals.

Step No. 3. Sort out priorities, giving the most imperative goal top position. Logically, top priorities take precedence over anything else; anything else on the list will, if necessary, be sacrificed to that goal. Facing that fact is very threatening to many people. They're like a puppy trying to claim two large bones at once; they can't bear to let anything go; therefore they keep shifting their choices. Perhaps you have a counselee who is married to an abusive but wealthy husband. At the top of the list she writes DIVORCE. Next on the list she writes FINANCIAL SECURITY. It may turn out she can have both, but if she really wants the divorce above all, she'll be willing to forego the financial security. Perhaps this woman has the two items reversed, else she would already have the divorce. Most people have trouble facing up to realistic priorities; they're influenced by their emotional needs, or the so-called standards of society, or someone else's opinion. Emotionally insecure people have an especially difficult time.

You may find people who give lip service to certain priorities but ignore them in actual practice, like the puppy who wags his tail gratefully when you give him his bone but later goes his own way, trying to grab up everything else in the dog pen. You're sure to witness this behavior, especially if you counsel alcoholics or overeaters or drug addicts. Some will eventually hang onto one good bone, the top priority on their written list, but it takes more behavior change than others of them can sum up. They want to exercise restraint, but their emotions pull them inexorably to that other bone which they've chewed on for a long time to gain a sense of security. Whenever you do find that an alcoholic, an overeater, or a drug addict has held on to this rational priority bone you'll feel like celebrating with Fourth of July fireworks!

Step No. 4. Identify the problem. This is done by checking the list of goals, because, remember, goals are always needs, that which the counselee needs in order to make life rewarding and worthwhile. Problems occur when one of these needs is not being met. This is a very simple principle, yet many people do not recognize it.

You will meet many people who complain about being unhappy, but they don't know why; they don't know what the problem is. They punch and jab at all kinds of scapegoats around them, the government, the younger generation, the weather, the overpopulation, but this blaming routine fails to make them any happier. For example, perhaps a person who's been retired for a time finds he's disappointed with the whole routine. He'd expected to enjoy a life filled with marvelous outings and hobbies and TV programs and lazing in bed. Now his life is filled with all those things, but they don't seem so marvelous. He's not enjoying them. If he were to make an accurate list of his needs, he'd probably include the need to feel worthwhile, a need which, for him, could be fulfilled only by doing something which he considered useful. He could probably cure his malady by finding a small part-time job, perhaps some vitally important volunteer work. With other people depending upon him for their well-being, he'd recover his sense of self-worth. But before he could solve his problem, he'd have to identify it.

One reason for identifying problems by looking at goals (needs) is that this method helps you to discriminate between your problems and someone else's problems. Many people needlessly complicate their lives by getting confused about who owns the problem. If you have a need that's not being filled, you have a problem. If someone else has a need that's not being filled he has a problem. Now you might try to involve him in helping you solve your problem, and if he wants to cooperate, that's fine. But don't try to put the problem onto him. On the other hand, don't go around taking on other people's problems, your children's, your friends', and so on.

Ann, a charming, loving friend of mine, shared with me her great relief and joy when she finally recognized this truth and began to practice it. For many years she'd been taking on other people's problems or trying to involve other people in hers. The futility of such behavior finally occurred to her so she immediately began acting accordingly. Her first opportunity occurred on the golf course. She was concentrating on a long drive, while some strangers standing nearby were being particularly distracting, shouting, laughing loudly and so on. She, with her new insight, now realized that she had a problem and would have to accept it as such. It was not the strangers' problem. She had two obvious choices. She could concentrate intensely enough to block out the erratic behavior going on around her, or she could ask for cooperation. If she did so, she'd have to admit her position. She might say, "Look, I have a problem. I can't concentrate when there's a lot of distraction." If the strangers wanted to become involved in her problem, they would quiet down, but she couldn't expect to force them to do so. She chose to concentrate on her drive, and, much to her delight, placed a long, low one about 190 yards down the fairway!

Mothers often get into the habit of taking on their children's problems. When young Sally needs a boyfriend, Mother is very likely to start rounding up every eligible male in the neighborhood. And when Junior needs to make a reputation in Little League, Mother is right out there yelling at the coach and the umpire. She can't understand that her behavior is not only humiliating but it deprives the kids of the opportunity to grow up. Most important, this shouldering of everyone's problems puts too much burden on her; she'll be old before her time.

Each person would find life simpler, more satisfying, and more harmonious if he learned to meet his own needs and let everyone else meet theirs.

Some people will insist they know what their problem is and want to begin right there, without listing goals; but usually their haste is wasteful, because they go far afield before getting on the right track. Sometimes their statement of the problem consists in naming a scapegoat—the boss who fired them, or the teacher who gave them a bad grade, or the immoral movies which led their daughter into a life of sin. One young man made an appointment with me which he later cancelled, explaining he didn't need me after all; he knew what his problem was and had now found another way to solve it. A little questioning revealed that the "other way" was a book on how to make a million dollars. I was extremely happy that he'd gone to another authority for that information. Thinking back on our conversation, I suspect that his real problem was a lack of self-esteem. I doubt if he can buy it for a million dollars.

Like goals, problems can also be stated in differing strata of importance. One's overall problem might be lack of love, but his immediate problem might be how to get a certain girl's telephone number. Or perhaps a person has several problems on the same level. A man trying to patch up a marriage might have to juggle several problems at once: how to communicate better with his wife, how to get a better job, and how to control his infidelity. Some problems are overlapping or interlaced. Often a client says to me, "I drink because I have a problem; I have no self-confidence." Very likely the statement is true, but until he controls the drinking, he won't gain the self-confidence. Alcoholics Anonymous understand this perfectly and work on both problems at once. Their members gain confidence in themselves by helping other people at the same time they are controlling their own drinking.

Step No. 5. Decide what action or actions can be taken, what choices are possible in order to solve the problem and attain the goal or goals.

I use the word "action" as well as the word "choice" because most persons think of problem solving as taking some action. Problem solving always involves a choice, but sometimes that choice is to take some action and sometimes the choice is to take no action at all, to leave everything just as it is.

The most common failures in problem solving are caused by the lack of imagination or wisdom to discover or create a wide spectrum of choices. Clients make such statements as, "I'll have to marry my pregnant girlfriend or go to jail." Or parents say, "Well, letting Junior drive a dangerous motorcycle is better than having him out robbing banks." They've gotten snared into an either-or pattern of choices and fail to look for additional alternatives.

You can encourage the counselee to adopt a kind of "think tank" method of looking for choices. For many years large companies have made a practice of having regular meetings wherein any idea which comes to mind, no matter how foolish it seems, is tossed out for consideration. There is never any criticism or ridicule, so originality and creativity are encouraged. Some of the greatest ideas in advertising and engineering and science have evolved out of this method. The person who accepts the principle of this brainstorming will learn to look at wide numbers of choices, acknowledging that most of them will not be useful, but some of them will probably be acceptable. Perhaps the counselee ought to be coerced to produce at least five alternative choices of action, no matter how inane they might seem, for each problem he wants to solve. That way he would learn to exercise his resourcefulness and creativity, his most valuable tools.

The brainstorm approach is especially useful for problems such as job-hunting. Many people get themselves locked in to one kind of work and can't imagine doing anything else, even though there are no jobs in that field available. If only they could overcome their prejudice against change, they could unfold a whole new world for themselves. The eminent psychologist Sydney Jourard calls this "re-inventing" oneself and believes it ought to be done several times in each lifetime. In a way, it's like being born again, since one will be thrown into a completely different circle of companions and life-styles. A client of mine who is in his fifties has recently changed his vocation from electronic engineering to real estate. He claims he's never been so happy. For the first time in his life, he is free to talk to people and to come and go as he likes. He's out of doors a great deal and feels healthier than he has for years. He's an outstanding example of a Jourardian "re-invention," and his decision to step into a new world was the result of a session much like the "think-tank" idea.

Another method of finding alternative choices is to observe how other people have chosen to solve the same problem. What choices, what behaviors overcome loneliness, financial insecurity, poor school grades, or whatever the problem might be?

For a few persons, Step 5 will carry them far enough to relieve their anxieties. Some people sink into desperate depressions because they feel trapped, helpless. They feel there's no way out of their dilemma, no alternatives available; for example, the wife and mother who's married to an alcoholic or to an intractable gambler, the father who loathes his job situation, the college student whose course of study, odious to him, was chosen by his parents. But these people may find that once they discover they really do have workable choices, their spirits are lifted and the circumstances become more bearable. With the depression alleviated they may decide it's wiser, for one reason or another, to continue in their present arrangement for a time, then exercise their final choices later. Or perhaps they'll never make those changes. Just knowing that alternatives are open to them, that they themselves are in control of their lives, gives them more peace of mind and sense of security.

Step No. 6. Examine and test each choice. In considering each alternative, the problem solver first asks himself the general question:

"What assumptions am I making? Could they be faulty?"

Then he examines the choices in a more detailed manner, for example,

1. Is this choice certain to gain for me what I want? Is it effective?
2. What other situations will it lead to?
3. How will the persons involved react? How will it affect them? How do I know?
4. Is it realistic?
5. Is it practical?
6. What are the risks involved? What are the drawbacks? What is the worst that could happen?
7. Would I be happier or unhappier than I am now?
8. Is it the choice or action of an authentic, mature person?

Some of these test questions seem to overlap, but each will be more or less applicable, depending upon the particular problem or choice being considered.

Emotionally insecure or immature persons are likely to be unrealistic in evaluating the possible outcome of their actions, guiding themselves mostly by wishful thinking. Not long ago a girl wrote to me, asking my opinion about a decision she'd made. She'd "borrowed" her mother's gold bracelet and then lost it. Now, rather than tell her mother what had happened, she'd decided to keep still and let everyone think the bracelet had been stolen so that the insurance company would pay for it. She believed that monetary compensation would put everything right again. Had she tested this choice, she might have found that she was making several possibly faulty assumptions. She assumed everyone would think a stranger had broken into the house and stolen the bracelet; it did not occur to her that an innocent friend or relative might be blamed. She assumed that the insurance company would settle without any investigation or tricky questioning which might entrap her. She assumed that her mother attached no sentiment to the bracelet so would be happy just to be paid for it. She assumed the parents' insurance policy would fully cover the bracelet, not allowing for deductibles which most policies provide for. She assumed her mother would not be forgiving if she, the girl, honestly confessed her foolish crime, expressing her pain and regret. The girl had questioned none of these assumptions, each of which had an important bearing on the case.

However, not only young children are unrealistic. A client of mine had grown resentful of his wife's continued nagging about the $1,500 he'd secretly loaned to his sister. The wife had eventually learned of the loan and knew it had never been repaid. She constantly harangued the husband to demand the money, which he would never do, realizing the sister's crippled financial state. On this particular day, he arrived in my office with a wonderful (or so he thought) plan for quieting his wife, once and for all. He would borrow the $1,500 and give it to his wife, claiming that he'd finally approached the sister about repaying the loan and had gotten the money. He believed that such a scheme would satisfy his wife and save his sister's honor. Of course the rather childish plot failed to stand up under any testing. It was unrealistic to think his wife would never discover the truth; but if she didn't, she would probably berate him for not requesting the money long before. She would assume the sister could have

paid it any time, but just didn't bother. It was also impractical to pay a high rate of interest on such a loan, not to
mention the probability that the wife might spend the money
rather carelessly, feeling it was almost a gift they didn't
expect to get anyway. Needless to say, the husband tossed
out the whole idea and chose another alternative, to ignore
the wife's nagging.

Step No. 7. Select and activate the most appropriate
choice. It goes without saying that several choices may attend
the same problem. A student who wants to improve his
grades may have to study more at home, pay stricter attention at school, not spend so much time on the telephone, stop
watching TV, and so on.

The other steps may have seemed somewhat confusing,
but this one is very difficult, because each alternative choice
probably has advantages and disadvantages which put the
counselee on the horns of that old devil—dilemma. Besides,
there is still the painfulness of change in full operation.

If you are using these steps as a "people-helper" this
stage of the problem solving process will also begin to test
your skill and patience. For one thing, you will be extremely
eager for the counselee to come to some decision and take
action, fearing that if he fails to do so within a certain length
of time, he will begin to distrust his own abilities and lapse
into a state of discouragement or limbo, getting nowhere. In
addition, you may be tempted to give advice rather than trust
the counselee to reach the wisest decision. You are afraid
that the woman who so much wanted the divorce will stay
with the abusive husband, or that the father will, after all,
have an affair, or that the alcoholic and overeater will not
let go of their security bones. You are dead certain you know
what's best for all of them and can hardly resist a little
meddling. But instead, you bite your tongue.

Don't be surprised if the overweight girl admits she'll
probably postpone dieting until after the Thanksgiving-
Christmas-New Year's holidays; after all, with all those
parties coming along, what can she do? Or the alcoholic gives
you a reason this week for not going to A.A., and another
reason next week, and another the week after that. Or the

woman with the abusive husband decides she'd probably get more alimony if she waited until Mr. Moneygrabber closed the next big deal. You can't force any of these people into action, but there are several things you can do.

First, you can prompt the counselees to go back and review steps numbers six and seven. It could be that they need to reconsider and reevaluate their choices and decisions. Perhaps Mrs. Moneygrabber will have to decide on a temporary separation at first, to ease her into divorce. Or perhaps the overeater has selected a diet much too ascetic or needs the support of a group like Weight Watchers. Or perhaps the alcoholic who so bravely chose to go to A.A. alone is scared to death and needs a friend to accompany him there.

Next, you can avoid letting the dependents, such as the overeater and the alcoholic, lean on you for support, week after week, which they might like to do instead of working on the solutions for their problems. And finally, you can be thankful for that one in four who makes it. In this case, the father, instead of plunging into an affair, has followed through with his decision to stay with his family and is making an appointment for professional joint family counseling next week. It gives you great satisfaction to realize that the problem solving procedure proved itself out very neatly in his case!

You are bound to feel sometimes that overwhelming desire to correct all the ills of the world and to be disappointed with anything less than one hundred percent effectiveness, but you must keep your expectations within limits. Of course, it's exasperating and discouraging to find that troubled people will not allow themselves to be helped, but it must be remembered that their emotions have woven powerful nets around their psyches so that their responses are almost beyond their control. To explain that they will be much happier if they let go of something their emotions want them to hang onto is like assuring a man at sea on a life raft that he will be happier if he jumps into the shark-infested water and swims five miles to shore. His emotional reflexes simply won't allow him to do it. At least not right away.

On the other hand, some of your counselees will eagerly

accept your help and will revise their whole life-style to make it more joyous and meaningful.

As a finale to this chapter, it would be appropriate to review the seven steps and then put one problem through the process.

The seven steps are: 1) Ventilating emotions; 2) Listing goals (needs, objectives), long-range, short-range; 3) Arranging priorities of goals; 4) Identifying problem; 5) Gathering alternative choices; 6) Testing choices; and 7) Selecting appropriate choice and taking action.

Previously, I referred to the boy Philbert, who was vacillating between taking his girl Patty to a hamburger stand or to a gourmet restaurant. Phil needs a rather quick decision, his date is this Saturday night. He's a well-adjusted guy who doesn't have real emotional hangups, so he buckles down to his problem solving immediately. His goals are arranged according to priority.

LONG-RANGE GOALS	SHORT-RANGE GOALS
1. Complete education and get established in meaningful work.	1. Make decisions where to take Patty on first date.
2. Love and be loved.	2. Keep finances at a safe level in order to complete education

PROBLEM: Where to take Patty to dinner.
CHOICES: (After brainstorming)
1. Take Patty to gourmet dinner.
   Approximate Cost - $40.00
2. Take Patty to hamburger stand.
   Approximate Cost - $ 5.00
3. Take Patty to Mom's house.
   Approximate Cost - $ 0.00
4. Take Patty on moonlight picnic at the beach.
   Approximate Cost - $ 5.00

TESTING OF CHOICES:
1. *Gourmet Dinner.* Assume Patty will be impressed. Perhaps not. May feel I am trying to show off. May

not appreciate fancy food. May lead to situation in which she'll always expect expensive dates and then later be disappointed. Not at all practical; would have trouble keeping to tight budget. Worst that could happen—she drops me, also, financial embarrassment. Education impaired. Am I being authentic? No! I'm not that rich!

2. *Hamburger Stand.* Assume Patty won't like it, I'm not certain. May lead to her dropping me because she thinks I've no "style" or am "tight." Also, she's probably tired of this dull routine; high-schoolish. Not very special. It's financially practical. Risks involved: may lose Patty, may have dull evening. Choice of authentic person? No, too much herd instinct.

3. *Taking Patty to Mother's.* Assume Patty will be flattered, but perhaps she'll think I'm rushing the "meet my folks" bit. Not certain to gain goal; may scare her off. On the other hand, may lead to quick engagement—too quick; I'm not ready. Practical financially. Risk: dull evening; folks good-hearted but not young. Also risky otherwise, see above. Not choice of real person; too much like mama's boy.

4. *Moonlight Picnic on the Beach.* Assume she likes beaches. Doesn't everyone? Romantic setting and I can show off my guitar. Ought to gain something. Hope it leads to more situations of the same. Very practical financially. Risks? Well, yes, but this kind I can handle. Choice of authentic person? You bet!

SELECTION OF CHOICE: Number Four
TAKING ACTION: Positively!

There's one aspect of problem solving I haven't touched upon, although it's very important to the counseling situation. Like everything else, a person sees a problem more clearly when he voices the problem and it's mirrored back to him. And once he sees it clearly, often the solution spontaneously occurs to him. Therefore, much of your assistance with problems, especially the small ones, will consist of reflective listening. I've proven this principle so often in my own life. At one time I worked closely with another counselor, Sarah. When I was baffled about how to handle a situation in my counseling practice, I would go next door and spill out the problem to her. Sarah was a genius at reflective listening, so it usually didn't take long for me to get some enlightenment. Much of the time the solution would occur to me almost before I'd finished telling. In fact, Sarah was such a good counselor that sometimes, after framing in my mind what I was going to say, the solution would occur to me by the time I reached her door!

Another important point in problem solving is not to stew about it endlessly. Instead, go through the steps up to the choice-making step, and then relax and drop it completely for a while, perhaps twelve hours. If you can completely relax, mentally and emotionally, during that period of time, you'll often find that the solution announces itself, loud and clear.

And one last comment: If the problem solver who intends to complete Step 7 does not follow through, does not take action, he must admit that he honestly does *not* want to solve the problem. As the poem states, he would "rather be ruined than change!"

Sometimes those persons who are immature or emotionally insecure believe that once they solve the present problem, life will be one big cornucopia of jamoca-almond-ice cream, or some other tasty dish. Perhaps the most valuable counseling you can do in the problem-solving process is to teach the counselee, in some tender way, that life is just a series of problems, more or less bothersome. We all have to face the fact that, on this earth at least, we can never just sit back and expect everything to run like syrup on a hot pancake. Some people live in a world of continuous "if only." "If only I could solve this one problem, I'd be happy." As soon as that problem is solved, another "if only" bubbles up to the surface. "If only I had this one thing, I'd be happy." These people waste their whole lives trying to eliminate the "if only's" instead of getting on with the business of enjoying life. A person who's in a good place emotionally, who feels strong, lovable, and capable will find each new problem to be a challenging segment of living. He'll take pride in his ability to put his problem-solving methods to work and will be eager to prove himself, in this real life game. He'll realize everyone must cope with his share of disappointment, even tragedy.

Psychologist George Kelley has had a lot to say about being prepared or not being prepared for the realities of life. He's based much of his personality theory on the idea of "constructs." Constructs are concepts you've built concerning the world, the way you think the world really is. Perhaps you've built a concept that blondes have more fun or that money brings happiness or that the world is flat. Most concepts can't be proven and most of them have been molded a great deal by emotional needs, but you accept them as true and live by them. To you they're the real world. Kelley explains that when life experience does not square with one of our concepts, you get all shaken up. For instance, a friend highly recommends a certain restaurant. It has a fancy name, fancy decor, and fancy sounding menus. You expect the food to be fancy, that's your concept; but it turns out to be the same old meat and potatoes you get at home. You're angry. In fact, you're extremely angry. Another night you're in a hurry and casually drop into the local beanery. The food is the same old meat and potatoes you get at home. You're pleased. In fact, you're extremely pleased. The food fits your concept.

It's the same with our expectations about life. If you expect it to be a gourmet dinner, everything perfect and no problems, you'll be disappointed. Too many unrealistic expectations can also cause intolerable frustration, anger, depression, emotional ills, and even criminal violence. But if you are realistic and expect beanery fare, with now and then a few problems, like a mouse in the beer[7] or lumps in the gravy, you can hang onto your equanimity and be pleased, extremely pleased!

Perhaps you're wondering if this attitude is in contradiction to the philosophy that a person who is emotionally secure, who is lovable and loved, sees the world as good and wonderful. What, then, is this about lumps in the gravy? There's no contradiction. Ask anyone who's in love. The lumps in the gravy taste just wonderful!

5.

Building Self-Identity Through Communication

All of us need to establish our authentic, individual identity. Without a strong sense of personal identification life is an unsatisfying muddle; we cannot feel poised and confident, we cannot make choices, we cannot set goals. Unless we each define ourselves, we cannot define our place in the world.

If you yourself need a stronger sense of identity you can begin by verbalizing your feelings and attitudes honestly but appropriately, a practice which, as you've already learned, helps to build a strong "I AM" consciousness, and gives you a feeling of potency and acceptance. This kind of verbalization helps in the task of shaping your unique Self, because as you sort out your feelings and attitudes in order to express them, you are making choices about who and what you are. Each statement you utter forces you to make a commitment, however temporary, which delineates a segment of your personality; each opinion you express defines a part of you.

Perhaps you will protest that as a thoughtful, private person who reads a great deal and thinks deep, clear thoughts, you can mold your own identity without the help of any very personal verbalizing. True, you may be an independent soul whose inspiration comes from within, and you may do a great deal of serious studying and meditating so that much of your self-creation is guided and influenced by a world far removed from social life. Many of your choices may be made by your own standards. But much of your identity is a composite of the social roles you play; few people exist forever as hermits. And you will find that unless you learn to express yourself, however succinctly and gently, your identity will be undeveloped or blurred. You will not know who you are.

In this search for Self, not only verbal expression, but also verbal interaction is an indispensable aid in clarifying the thought processes. You can't know exactly how or what you think or feel until you put it all into words and then compare and contrast other persons' reactions to those words. With this interaction you encounter both what you are and what you could be if you decide to change yourself. You are confronted by society's demands on you and how you accommodate or compromise those demands. Only through this community process can you grow; without it you cannot become an authentic person.

For most people, free discussion illuminates areas they never knew existed, especially if they're courageous enough to explore and learn to express the emotions, both the positive and negative ones, in a calm nondefensive manner. The emotions are the very basis of the Self, so unless one gets down to that level, identifies it, analyzes it, understands it, and expresses it, he cannot feel that he is authentic. He cannot get the feel of "I AM." He cannot become a real person because he cannot make logical, constructive decisions. His emotions, which he won't even be aware of, much less understand, will pull him this way and that. Like a blind swimmer, he may really be pulled out to sea, while firmly believing he is making his way safely to shore.

However important the emotions may be, in ordinary conversation there's very little talk on this level. Most of the chit-chat going on around us centers on trivial facts: "I bumped into ole' Charlie on the street today." "Oh, yeh? What's he doin'?" "Nothin' much, I guess." "Oh." Or it's about trivial opinions: "I see in the paper the government is going to raise taxes! They ought to close up about half of those fancy schools. The darn kids don't learn much anyhow and that way we'd save a bundle." Or the talk concerns trivial domestic events: "I took that dress back to the cleaners again. They still didn't get the spot out."

Communication on this level is no more than a buzz, like the static of a radio that's left on without being tuned in. Or like the ticking of a clock put into a puppy's bed to keep it company. Even while engaging in such small talk, the persons would have a larger dimension if they got down to the emotions, such as, "I always loved good ole' Charlie," or "I feel panicky when I hear that taxes are going to be raised; I can't afford it," or "I really get annoyed when the cleaners do a poor job." Not only would the statement have more meaning but the speakers themselves would feel more alive and real. Further, relationships would improve because people would finally become mindful of one another's emotional needs and sensitive to one another's pain and joy. True understanding comes of knowing the emotions, for emotions color all our thinking, no matter how computerlike people attempt to be.

Seldom can anyone see an issue or situation or even a philosophic principle from a strictly objective, disinterested standpoint. (A woman once wrote to me, "My husband, a clearheaded engineer, gets *furious* when you claim his opinions are colored by his emotions." Perhaps he didn't consider fury to be an emotion.) Whenever a discussion grows heated or strained, emotions are obviously involved and in such cases reason usually flies out the windows. Most persons have a great deal of ego identity invested in their religious, political, or philosophical points of view. No amount of logic could dislodge them and any attempt to do so is a threat which arouses strong emotion.

Certainly, the evaluation of any situation, whether it occurs in personal life or in the world at large, is viewed through an emotional bias tinted by individual belief systems, prejudices, and warped impressions. Most people are unaware of these emotions, mostly because they've not dug them out and taken a good look at them. Or because their ego involvement is so deep, they dare not be honest and frank about their emotions. Instead, they escape into long dissertations and explanations.

One reason people don't try to identify and express their feelings is that they've learned not to. Small children might want to walk up to a friend and say, "I like you," but with our system of child rearing it doesn't take long for them to build up all kinds of doubts about themselves and reach the place where they can't afford to risk rejection. Then they don't dare say "I like you" for fear that someone who's been brought up in the same system and has his own problems might reply, "Buzz off and stop buggin' me, Kid." With all the doubts about themselves already growing, this kind of rebuff would be agonizing. It would just reinforce what they'd already begun to suspect, that they aren't worth much. They're not worth being liked.

Another reason people don't express feelings is that society has frowned upon it as being bad form. Warm affectionate feelings have been considered "gushy." Recently a client in my office said she'd completed Jess Lair's book which recommends saying, "I love you" to five people. I asked if she'd completed that assignment and she said no. She'd said it to her three children, but not to her husband because she wasn't getting along very well with him, and not to anyone else. Many times previously she'd told me of her deep devotion to her father; she adored him. At the time, she was worried because she'd been told he had cancer. In view of her affection and her worry, I gently asked if she could tell her father that she loved him. As her throat tightened and the tears rolled down her cheeks, she managed to gasp, "No, it would be too embarrassing." Thank the gods, we are gradually reaching the point where few families inhibited!

Even more than the feelings of love, our society forbidden the feelings of fear, hate, or anger. From the time we're very little boys and girls, we're told that it's cowardly to feel afraid and it's naughty to harbor hate or anger; good little boys and girls don't have such "bad" feelings and if we show we have them, we'll be punished. Actually, anger has been given to us by Mother Nature as a defense; it's what makes us get up and fight back after someone knocks us down emotionally. Our culture has been very cruel to us about anger. It has said, "We're going to create in you all kinds of hurts and guilts and fears, but then we are not going to allow you to have the anger which you need to fight off the depression those emotions would otherwise cause." It's like binding a person to a bed and then giving him the hotfoot.

We're told to control anger, but nobody tells us how. It's really no use to tell it to go away. What we often do is put it someplace where it causes great harm. Sometimes we put the fear and tension and anger into our own bodies, where they cause serious illness.

Some very maladjusted people channel their anger in another way, in a malicious or sneaky way, making everyone around them miserable. Criminals are usually very hurt, insecure angry people, their self-esteem at rockbottom. Other people, while not actually preying upon society, are in a constant bad temper, hiding their anger behind blaming, criticizing, backbiting, or perhaps self-righteous moralizing. But some people are more subtle; they hide their anger behind manipulations, controlling those around them by arousing guilt. Usually these people don't dare admit their anger openly or even to themselves. They continue to siphon it down deep inside, into a secret "anger pot" with a tight lid, where it seethes and ferments, and sometimes finally explodes. The explosion may be only an uncontrollable temper tantrum, or it may be a violent crime.

Everyone would do well to learn how to accept and handle the strong, negative feelings which most people are bound to experience in this stressful world. True, there are a few rare souls who appear to be so emotionally secure that they never feel threatened by the inevitable "slings and arrows." They understand the strengths and frailties of their fellow humans, as well as their own. If anyone threatens them, they wonder what his problem is. In general, they see themselves as worthwhile and the world as a pretty good, safe place. But a larger part of our society are not that secure. They suffer feelings of humiliation, guilt, frustration or rejection, and then the anger builds. They can find no satisfying method of relief, of letting go.

Some people know that it would make them feel better to express their negative emotions, but they resist this tactic not only because they've been taught not to do so, but because they're afraid that the ugly feelings will pop out violently and noxiously, thereby damaging some cherished interpersonal relationship. They don't realize that if one does not allow his fiery feelings to build up, but instead adopts the habit of confronting them tolerantly as they occur, accepting them as an aspect of humanness, and examining them openly, he finds such emotions easier to handle. He can then express the anger in a calmer, more subdued, less hurtful manner. He can express the anger and assume full responsibility for it, without blaming those around him. No one minds the expression of anger. Everyone minds being blamed for it.

However, people who haven't known how to dissipate their anger as it occurs over the years so that it's left to fester within them would do well to practice some kind of rage reduction. There are many techniques. Some therapists advise their patients to use punching bags, or to jab pillows, all the time pretending the bag or pillow is the source of their anger. Other therapists recommend strenuous sports or athletic exercise which will supposedly dissipate the anger. Others recommend an aggressive action, like chopping wood, which takes the place of the punching bag activity, but with a more violent connotation and no wasted effort. I've never subscribed to any of these methods, even though some frustrated, angry persons might find them very effective.

My own type of rage reduction entails verbalizing the anger in a strong, loud, aggressive manner. I believe that we are verbal creatures, and that we feel most effective, most positive, when we are expressing ourselves on that level. Poking a pillow is more appropriate behavior for an animal, perhaps an enraged bull. It doesn't say much about the anger; it doesn't declare the full power of a thinking, vocal human being.

The verbalizing shouldn't take place in the presence of anyone else, not even the object of the anger. The angered person should find a place where he's safely alone; preferably a place where there's other noise so he won't feel self-conscious about the loudness of his own voice, perhaps in the shower with the water on full force, or in a parked car near the ocean or a waterfall. Some people perform their rage reduction routine while driving along a freeway. In a traffic emergency they quickly stop the yelling. The sound of the motor drowns out their voice, and other motorists just think they're rehearsing a play or singing. (If you don't feel this is against safety regulations, go ahead. It's probably no more distracting than other common practices by motorists, such as trying to control unruly kids or arguing violently with a spouse.) Other people don't mind hearing themselves yell out their rage, so they just find any place where they can be alone.

Once the person decides to use this method, he should really let go with his total lung power, summoning up all the anger he can muster, using the very strongest language he knows. And I mean the very strongest language. He should think of all the people in his whole lifetime who've caused him any kind of hurt or humiliation or who have rejected him in any way: teachers, parents, friends, salespeople, head-waiters, or whatever. Then really give it to them! This should be done for about four minutes a day for a while. But he shouldn't expect immediate results. If he goes through this procedure daily for a couple of weeks, and after that occasionally, as he feels he needs it, one day he'll suddenly realize he isn't very angry any more. He may vaguely try to remember what upset him so much. He'll have a more toler-ant, accepting feeling toward the targets of his anger and toward the world in general, not only because he has ventilated the anger, but because he has validated himself.

Despite the fact that this routine is very simple and harmless, you'd be surprised how many mixed up persons simply cannot bring themselves to carry it out. They squirm around with all kinds of excuses. They protest they don't have any anger inside them, despite the fact they've just talked to me for several hours about all the hate which is galling them and distorting their whole view of life. Or they protest that it's wrong to shout ugly words, despite the fact they're probably ruining their own or their family's lives with their ugly, neurotic, manipulative behavior. They've been so enculturated against expressing strong anger that they simply can't admit, even to me, that they're capable of such violent expressions. Often they can be very honest about much more reprehensible acts, perhaps cheating on their spouses, or reading their daughter's secret diary, or running up a lot of debts which they'll never be able to pay, or running out on a girl they've gotten pregnant. But they can't sit in a car and shout their defiance, the thing they need to do the most!

Some therapists suggest that the patient meet with the people he considers the cause of his anger and just "let it all out," violent words and all. They explain, "Be honest. Say whatever you think. Clear the air." I don't believe for a minute that it clears the air. A storm like that does just about as much good as a cyclone; it might blow away a bit of garbage, but it also might wreck a few homes. Usually the offending person or persons are relatives, like mothers and fathers, who've done the very best they knew how; but the offspring hasn't matured enough to realize that parents are only human. Besides, suppose the offending person is one's employer? Or someone who now lives a thousand miles away? Or someone out of touch, perhaps dead. Furthermore, usually one session of rage reduction is not enough, but one can't keep spewing out his rage to the same person over and over again! All in all, the personal attack method is dangerous, impractical, and ineffective. The strong, by yourself, verbal venting is the most effective.

INVENTORY OF FEELINGS

The following is a partial list of feelings. Because so much depends upon context, it is difficult to categorize feelings. However, this list helps to make us aware of the many shadings of emotions so that we can sort them out for ourselves.

Loving
affectionate
agreeable
amiable
ardent
caring
compassionate
concerned
congenial
cooperative
enraptured
fond
friendly
gentle
sensual

Brave
calm
confident
courageous
fearless

Accepted
appreciated
approved of
attractive
fulfilled
gratified

Peaceful
carefree
contented
refreshed
relaxed
released

relieved
resigned
safe
satisfied
secure

Amused
charmed
delighted
entertained
pleased

Blissful
bubbly
cheerful
ecstatic
elated
enthralled
euphoric
excited
exhilarated
festive
glad
gleeful
happy
jolly
joyful
jubilant
lively
marvelous
merry
overjoyed
rapturous
rejoicing

thrilled

Detached
apathetic
lethargic
listless
remote

Blocked
baffled
caged
frustrated
oppressed
shackled
suffocated
trapped

Drained
exhausted
lazy
overburdened
overwhelmed
sluggish

Bewildered
amazed
astonished
befuddled
confounded
confused
dazed
disoriented
dumbfounded
flabbergasted
flustered

Feelings, continued . . .

mixed up
muddled
mystified
perplexed
rattled
stumped
stunned

Apprehensive
afraid
alarmed
anguished
anxious
bothered
chicken
cowardly
fearful
frantic
frightened
nervous
terrified
uncertain
uneasy
up tight
worried

Ashamed
apologetic
belittled
chagrined
conscience-stricken
embarrassed
guilty
humiliated
insulted
mortified
regretful

Dejected
depressed
desolate
desperate
despondent
devastated
disappointed
discouraged
dismayed
despairing
dispirited
distraught
distressed
disturbed
downhearted
gloomy
grieved
hopeless
lonely
melancholy
miserable
moody
pained
perturbed
sad
sorrowful

Rejected
abandoned
abused
beaten
betrayed
bugged
cheated
crushed
cut off
deceived
defenseless

disgraced
disillusioned
estranged
forlorn
forsaken
friendless
harassed
heartbroken
hurt
intimidated
left out
let down
mistreated
misunderstood
neglected
offended
picked on
plagued
scorned
snubbed
victimized

Angry
aggressive
agitated
antagonistic
bitchy
bitter
defensive
defiant
disagreeable
disgusted
displeased
fuming
furious
grouchy
grumpy
hateful

hostile	irritated	rebellious
incensed	mad	resentful
indignant	peeved	riled
irate	provoked	surly
irked	quarrelsome	outraged

Miscellaneous Feelings

altruistic	prideful
benevolent	proud
bored	resolute
defeated	restless
eager	rewarded
firm	righteous
horrified	shocked
impatient	surprised
pensive	thoughtful
pessimistic	uninterested

Once a person feels his strong feelings are under control, he can begin the practice of sending daily messages about his emotional reactions. But before he can communicate an emotion, he must be able to identify it and put it into words. Very often people fail to understand this simple point. When asked how they feel about an event or about a person, they're likely to answer something like, "Oh, the State Fair was very large; it had many farm animal exhibits and must have made money," or "May is a good cook and housekeeper; she makes a good baloney sausage too," or "The hostess was probably inconvenienced because we left early," or "My son is learning to be a mortician." Of course, none of these statements answers the question, "How do you *feel* about . . .?" None expresses a single, solitary emotion. The speakers could have reached an emotional level had they said something like, "I enjoyed the exhibits of pigs and goats at the State Fair, but the crowds made me jittery," or "I admire May for her many abilities, but her competence sometimes makes me self-conscious," or "I felt guilty about leaving the party early," or "I'm relieved that my son is now learning a skill."

One of my clients, a very cold, tense woman who was trying to decide whether or not to leave her husband, was accused by him of never expressing herself clearly. He claimed she always spoke in innuendos, then expected him to read her mind. She denied this accusation, protesting he always knew exactly how she felt. As the counseling session progressed, she pointed out an example of her clear communication. The previous day, a Sunday, she had gotten up and gone into the kitchen to prepare breakfast. Her husband later followed her in, thinking to help her. For a long while she refused to answer anything he said but finally blurted out, "Leave me alone!" She cited this example triumphantly, adding, "You see? He knew exactly how I felt!" Now "Leave me alone" could ambiguously imply "I'm too busy to talk," "My hangover is killing me," "I don't want you to see me putting strychnine in your food," or a dozen other different meanings. Anyone with an active imagination could infer some pretty interesting implications. But "Leave me alone," all by itself is simply an order. It doesn't state anything resembling an emotion. The woman could have communicated her feelings clearly had she said something like, "I don't know why, but I'm feeling depressed and unsociable right now. Suppose you let me get breakfast alone. Perhaps I'll feel better after we eat." And she probably would feel better almost immediately because of verbalizing her emotion.

Often you'll find that the ventilation of negative feeling is instant therapy. The amateur speaker suffering from stage fright would do well to admit to a friend, or even to his audience, "I wanted to appear so cool and polished, but now my heart is pounding and my throat is dry. I guess I'm scared." Most likely the feelings of fear would then disappear, or at least lessen markedly.

It's not only important that the speaker identify and express the emotion accurately, but that he avoid putting the blame for his emotion onto someone else, especially the listener. I've created a little parable to illustrate the principle that one's emotions are his own, that the way he reacts to situations depends upon his own emotional stance.

Johnny, aged twelve, is standing on the corner, obviously in a foul mood, cussing out everyone who comes along. The first person to pass by is Johnny's mother. She's a timid, pious woman who promptly moans, "Oh, Johnny, how could you! You know you're taking the Lord's name in vain and that He'll probably punish us all, the whole family!" Her response is fear. Then Johnny's father comes along. He pleads, "What will the neighbors think? Suppose my boss should see you?" His response is shame. Then Johnny's best friend comes along. He observes Johnny for a while and then demands, "Gosh darn! How do you get by with that? If I did that, I'd get whaled!" His response is envy. Next, Johnny's grandfather, an old war veteran, comes along. He encourages, "Go on, Johnny, give it to em! That's the way my old sergeant used to talk. That proves you're a real man." His response is pride. A little later, Johnny's sister, who absolutely adores him, comes along. Immediately she bursts into tears as she cries, "Oh, Johnny, I love you so much. How could you do this to me?" Her response is heartbreak. Then Johnny's grandmother, a loving, wise old woman, comes along. She listens carefully to Johnny a few minutes and then declares, "Poor Johnny, he has a problem," and takes him into her arms.

Now Johnny didn't force anyone to feel anything. Each person responded according to his own personality structure and emotional bias, just as we all do. None of us can say, "You made me mad," or "You made me cry." It's the insecurity within us which allows such feelings. We've all had the experience of dealing with a grumpy salesperson, or a sulky hair stylist, or a waspish waiter, but we're foolish and childish to let that person dictate where we'll be "at" emotionally. Granted, continual unpleasantness is not easy to cope with; it's tiresome, stultifying, and boring. But even the wife who is married to a husband who constantly finds fault, or the husband who is married to a wife who constantly whimpers can, if emotionally secure, live fairly serenely, realizing, like Grandmother, that a loved one has a problem. In the final analysis each person is responsible for his own emotional response. Of course, if his companion is too unpleasant, he may opt for a change, but he will do it objectively, without feeling severe personal defeat. Life invariably deals out a series of disappointments but the secure person functions with courage and a realistic perspective.

Some counselors have hit upon a little device to force whoever is expressing himself in any emotionally charged discussion to accept responsibility for his own feelings and to avoid any blaming tactics. It's called "giving 'I' messages." The speaker sticks to what "I" think or do or feel; in that way he doesn't shift the blame onto the "You" involved. Usually "You" messages, especially the ones beginning with "You always," or "You never," simply turn the statement into a gambit for an ugly argument. Furthermore, the message has more clarity, more impact, and more authority if it not only centers upon the emotions, but states those emotions overtly rather than to depend upon the listener to infer them. On the other hand, communication always breaks down when it attempts to dissect and argue petty facts. This picking the sand out of the pepper ploy is bound to turn into a childish "he-did-he-didn't" seesaw. A few examples will demonstrate the difference between the two approaches.

"You" messages

Customer: You're always so slow in this restaurant; you'll make my wife and me infuriated if we're late to see the play. Besides, you didn't get my order straight.

Waiter: You'll have to take your turn like everybody else. I brought exactly what you ordered.

Customer:	You've put us in a bad mood and spoiled our whole evening.
Waiter:	You haven't helped mine much either.

"I" messages

Customer:	My wife and I have a problem. We're trying to get to the play by 8:30 and will be disappointed if we're late. Can you help us?
Waiter:	I'll try. It's crowded, but if you order something already prepared, like the prime rib, I think I can serve you quickly.
Customer:	Fine, we'll take that. We like prime rib.
Waiter:	Good. I hope you enjoy the play.

*****

"You" messages

Teacher:	You are so annoying! You never listen or follow instructions on the assignments; this paper is not what you were told to do.
Student:	You always garble your words, so how do I know what to do? You make me feel dumb.
Teacher:	You just don't have any interest in learning. You've earned no better than a "D."
Student:	You just don't like me and don't want me in your class.

*****

"I" messages

Teacher:	I'm disappointed in your paper. Evidently I didn't make my instructions clear enough.
Student:	Gee, I feel awful. I worked hard on that and thought for sure I'd get a good grade. I guess I got confused.
Teacher:	I'd really like to help you do better. Can you stop a minute after class? Perhaps you can improve your grade by just doing a little revising.
Student:	Gee, thanks. I'll do that.

*****

"You" messages

1st Neighbor:	You always let your dogs and kids run all over

my place and ruin my flowers and lawn. You never have any consideration for anyone else! You make me so mad!

2nd Neighbor: You make me mad too. You never remember that when you moved here it was already a family neighborhood. Now you expect us to lock up our kids just to please you.

1st Neighbor: You're irresponsible and slovenly. It would serve you right if I called the police.

2nd Neighbor: You've always been a mean old biddy, so you'll always cause trouble for us.

"I" messages

1st Neighbor: I really love kids and pets, but it upsets me to have my beautiful lawn and flowers ruined by your small boys and their dogs. Can you help me do something about it?

2nd Neighbor: Gosh, I'm surprised to know they're ever on your property. I hadn't noticed. Give me a day or two to discuss it at home.

1st Neighbor: I'd be thankful if we could arrange something to satisfy both of us. Perhaps we need some fencing.

2nd Neighbor: I'm sure we can work something out. Don't worry.

*****

"You" messages

Husband: You always ruin my evening because you never have dinner ready on time! You expect me to work all day and then go hungry. Why can't you be better organized?

Wife: You really get to me! You never let me know what time you're coming home, and then you complain.

Husband: You always have some excuse. You probably spent all your time gossiping on the phone, instead of doing your work.

Wife: There you go, trying to run my whole life!

"I" messages

Husband: Gee, I'm hungry as a bear. Is dinner ready? I was hoping it would be.

Wife: Oh, no. I'm terribly sorry, really. Here're a few snacks, cheese and crackers and stuff, to tide you over. I promise I'll hurry.

Husband: I like to have dinner as soon as I get home, but I guess I didn't tell you my schedule today. Oh well, the snacks will help. I'd like a cool drink too.

Wife: I'll fix it pronto! I love you for being so patient.

Some clients claim that their spouses never listen to them. Usually a lack of communication indicates that the husband or wife, whoever is accused of being deaf to all attempts at conversation, has experienced many previous discussions which involved a lot of accusing, exhorting, warning, and other painful put-downs. One woman, whose counseling sessions consisted of endless verbal attacks upon her husband, felt extremely resentful because he spent hours on the telephone listening to his employees' problems but, she charged, refused to listen to her feelings for even one minute. Apparently her husband enjoyed helping people and listened to many strong feelings poured out to him, but he didn't enjoy being blamed, criticized, and cut down. If the wife had stuck to "I" messages, accepting the responsibility for her own emotions, and then asked for his help, he might have felt the concern for her that he felt for his employees.

If your household has grown to expect that most conversations end up in bitter argument, the shift from noxious "You" messages to innocuous "I" messages may not be accepted and understood just overnight. It may take time to change the pattern of behavior. Before stating your feelings, you may have to reassure your listener, very convincingly, that you aren't out to do battle. You might begin by saying, "Now, I know this is my problem. I just want your help," or "Believe me, this is not your fault." Even so, your mate is likely to bang right back at you with a purely reflex action of defenses, counter accusations, and so on. Remember, we've all had so much experience with being blamed for someone else's feelings that we've become very adept at grabbing our guns and firing back at the first sign of attack. When your spouse shoots you down before he sees your white flag, you'll just have to fall back on your reflective listening, in order to keep the situation from becoming a full-scale battle. For example:

"I" message
Husband: It's not your fault, but I'm really not enjoying this party very much. I'd like to go home.

Defense:
Wife: You're probably jealous because I'm having such a good time.

Reflective Listening:
Husband: So you're having a good time, eh? Wonderful! I guess I can hold out a little longer. Suppose we compromise and leave in an hour.

*****

"I" message:
Father: I know it's not your problem, but I'm expecting some business calls and I'm getting edgy because the phone is tied up.

Defense:
Daughter: Don't blame me! Can I help it if my friends call? You just don't approve of my friends.

Reflective Listening:
Father: You feel I'm blaming you for something that's not your fault. Let's talk this out a bit more. I'm sure we can see each other's point of view. But right now it's important that the phone is left free.

*****

If you are truly willing to suspend judgment and blame, eventually the conversations should go something like this:

"I" message:
Husband: I'm really not enjoying this party very much. I'd like to go home.

Wife:	I'm sorry you're having a dull time. Could you stand it for about ten more minutes? I want to hear more about Jan's trip.
Husband:	O.K., it's a deal.

*****

"I" message

Father:	I'm expecting some important business calls and I'm getting edgy because the phone is tied up for so long. Could you hang up and let those calls come through? I wouldn't mind if you used the phone later.
Daughter:	All right, Dad, if you gotta have it. Give me just a couple of minutes, O.K.?
Father:	I appreciate that.

*****

A few warnings to keep you from falling into the Slough of Despond before you get onto the road. You'll have to guard against letting those old "You" messages slip into the conversation dressed up as "I" messages. Such statements as "I feel upset when you play that stupid music so loud and drop your bubble gum on the floor and leave your junk all over the garage, expecting me to clean it up," are nothing but "You" messages incognito. The exhorting and criticizing come through ever so clearly.

Also, it's extremely difficult not to get trapped into headtrips. When you're returning the ill-fitting new pair of shoes you just bought and a very unpleasant floor man sniffs, "What do you expect! Obviously, you've worn them already," it's hard to resist a vehement denial. However, you'll be much more effective if you simply reply, "I'm feeling very frustrated and annoyed. I'd expected this transaction to take only a minute." That will probably terminate the discussion. No one can argue with a feeling message; the person experiencing the feeling is the final authority. At home, when you want to get some particular feelings into the open but no one wants to hear about them, but wants to argue instead, it's even more difficult to resist the headtrips. Your mate may blast, "By the way, I really don't believe your story about why you didn't get home from the Marching and Chowder

Society until 2:00 A.M.." You might try something like, "Please, can we talk about that later? I'd really like to share some important feelings with you because I think then we'll understand each other better." Or you might drop back into reflective listening. If neither tactic avoids friction (and face it, sometimes nothing works), you may want to ease away from any attempt at communication for the time being and watch an old rerun on TV. Even if you don't get the opportunity at that moment to verbalize your feelings, your accurate recognition of them, even to yourself, is of valuable personal benefit. Sometimes you just have to be your own listener.

Another warning, you'll have to be sensitive as to when another person has the floor first. If you're attending a dinner party, and another guest is off and running, expressing some strong feelings, you'd best not try to compete. In fact, being very aware of the situation, you should drop into the active listening routine. The same at home. If you're a parent and your spouse or kids are having their turn at establishing their egos, there's no use to try to shout them down. Again you should turn on your active listening button.

The subject of shouting suggests another warning. Be sure that your statements reflect the true level of feelings, without underdoing or overdoing the violence or whatever happens to be your mood. If a mother says very softly to a child, "I don't like to be bitten," the message undershoots the true feelings. The child probably won't get the message. If the mother uses a more resolute tone, saying, "Ouch, I really don't like to be bitten. It hurts!" the child is more likely to understand the message accurately. However, if the mother is outraged and screams, "Dammit! Cut that out! You're killing me!" the mother overshoots and destroys the effectiveness of the communication by confusing and frightening the child.

For several reasons young people often get into the habit of overshooting. For one thing, they feel the insecurity of being small and weak and not in control of their own lives; therefore, any frustration or rejection arouses overly strong emotions which seem inappropriate, especially to adults, to the actual circumstances. Also, the strength of expression serves to compensate for the feelings of unimportance and impotence. Another reason for their overshooting is that they've not acquired the judgment to give each incident in their lives its proper importance or unimportance; a broken fingernail is as distressing as a broken leg. As they gain maturity and self-esteem, they can correct the overshooting, dropping their intensity of expression down to its appropriate level.

The manner in which we express our emotions is also a matter of cultural influence and often causes cultural gaps, misunderstandings among people of different backgrounds. For instance, Americans are accustomed to a degree of frankness in expressing their feelings. If a hostess prepares a lavish dinner for us, we are prone to compliment her on every detail, ohing and ahing over every dish. On the other hand, in the same circumstances the English might make no comment except a tight-lipped, "Good show," as they leave the house. To Americans, that's undershooting. Paula Prentiss, the actress, tells of a different experience. The first time that her husband, Dick Benjamin, took her home to meet his parents, she was grieved to see and hear what was happening. Afterward on the way to her apartment, she said to Dick, "What a shame about your parents; that terrible fighting! Are they going to get a divorce?" Dick answered, "Fighting? Who's fighting! In a Jewish home, that's dinner!" To Miss Prentiss, the parents were overshooting. Understanding the emotional reactions of various peoples is difficult. When their country is invaded, the Hollanders endure the rigors and deprivations of war in stolid silence. When their country wins the international bicycle races, the Italians sound as though they're staging a revolution.

People who constantly undershoot or overshoot in expressing their feelings among their friends and relatives finally begin to feel ineffective. They don't present themselves accurately to the world, so they don't get the appropriate feedback. The person who understates his feelings begins to feel that no one is listening, while the person who overstates them gets into overemotional situations unnecessarily. Expressing the precise intensity of feelings is almost as important as expressing the precise kind of feelings.

Most of this chapter has been devoted to the negative emotions, not because they're the most important, but because they cause the most grief and people need to learn how to handle them. Actually, people also need to learn how to handle the positive emotions, like love, joy, bliss, courage, contentment, compassion, and so on. For various reasons, many people go through life either in a state of foggy emotional insensitivity, unaware of such emotions, or they don't dare express them when they find them. Of all the many people I know who've read Jess Lair's directive to say to five people, "I love you," very few of them could complete the assignment. Like the daughter who could not say "I love you" to her own father, they are unable to gather the courage. Usually these people think, as did the daughter, the experience would be a source of embarrassment; but I've never ever known anyone to be embarrassed by being told "I love you." It's true that sometimes people are confused by the statement. It's a comment on our culture that most persons have heard the phrase so seldom that they don't know what to do with it, how to respond. They hesitate to return the sentiment, thinking such turnabout sounds insincere, like a woman who gets a compliment on her hairdo, then acknowledges the favor by saying, "I like yours, too." They haven't rehearsed any clever, polite answer, so are put off balance, growing vague and confused. But they're not embarrassed. Embarrassment is triggered by a feeling of having goofed, but hearing the statement "I love you" doesn't make anyone feel he's goofed.

Fortunately, in the bloom of our present Romantic Revolution, many persons are learning to say "I love you." Greeting card companies are selling I-love-you's by the million. Perhaps sending a greeting card instead of expressing a sentiment directly makes a person feel a little safer; he can hide behind the inference that he had a limited choice. If the recipient should happen to feel the card's a bit too mushy, he can blame the author. Furthermore, the picture on the card might lighten up the tone, so that the word "love" sounds rather casual. Unfortunately, unlike other languages, English has a scarcity of vocabulary in the love department; it's awkward and frustrating to have to get along with only one word to express the whole spectrum of feelings the verb could imply.

However, we don't verbalize any kind of positive emotion as much as we should or could. We find it difficult to express even a simple little emotion like joy. It's as though there's a kind of superstition about expressing joy, as if a bad witch might come along and take it away if we admitted we had it. Or that it's discourteous to boast about possessing such a valuable commodity, thereby making less fortunate people feel envious. But probably it's that many of us have gotten out of the habit of looking for the positive emotions and wouldn't feel skilled enough to express them, even if we found them.

Expression of emotion helps to establish our most real Self, so we need to give outlet to all nature of feelings, the happiness as well as the hurt. If we get up in the morning feeling wonderfully in harmony with the whole miracle of creation, we will feel more alive, more vital, if we express that glad music within us.

However much the importance of communicating feelings is explained, many persons still hesitate to do so. They feel that removing their thick masks of dispassion will make them vulnerable; their real selves will be revealed for inspection and their real selves will not measure up. They forget that the person who is gentle yet dares to be himself is admired; he appears strong and confident. What's more, the natural person seems more human, more approachable, more lovable, less of a fake. People feel closer to him, and his interpersonal relationships are more significant. Furthermore, dropping false pretenses is wonderfully relaxing and restful. It takes constant vigilance and a lot of emotional energy to keep a large mask from slipping out of place. It's a relief to throw it away.

Although this chapter urges the practice of self-expression it certainly does not advocate that the pursuit of self-expression should become such a continuous, ongoing practice that it leads to the development of extreme extroversion. The extremely extroverted personality style has been much overrated in the past forty years, ever since the Swiss psychoanalyst, Carl Jung, coined the terms "extrovert" and "introvert." Through a misunderstanding Americans have come to believe that introversion indicates an ugly self-centeredness leading to a twisted, secretive existence, whereas extroversion indicates an angelic love of people, so the more of it the better.

To throw light on the true, core meanings of the terms, it may be said that *introverts derive their life inspiration from within, whereas extroverts derive their life inspiration from without.* An extreme of either style is unhealthy.

If too introverted, a person does not learn social skills; he never interacts easily, so he feels self-conscious and awkward. He cannot develop a complete identity because he never learns the art of self-expression or active listening; he does not "process" himself, person-to-person. On the other hand, if too extroverted, a person becomes immaturely dependent on people, socially and emotionally. He must always be surrounded by friends and feels the need of them so that he must always be seeking approval in some form or another in order to win over and increase his social circle. This activity is apt to take so much of his time that he cannot devote enough attention to other endeavors in order to enrich and round out his life. Often he grows manipulative and dishonest in relationships, because he cannot bear disapproval or criticism. And usually, at least away from home, he must bury his anger or differences of opinion. He can never be an autonomous, real person. Of course, these are generalized behaviors; each individual reacts somewhat differently, depending on many variables.

Because extroversion has been so highly touted, children are criticized if they want to be selective in their choices of friends or if they enjoy spending time alone. They are prey to incessant propaganda: "People who need people are the luckiest people in the world." No one points out that people who love and are loved are, indeed, lucky. But people who "need" people, whose security is dependent upon others, are very unlucky! Like dependent drug addicts, they are enslaved, unable to grow. Fritz Perls defines maturity as the ability to function securely independent of the environment.

Common sense dictates that everyone should aim for a fair balance, at the same time allowing his natural, inborn inclination to dominate. Some individuals are naturally more introverted, some more extroverted, and both styles, if not extremes, can be useful and comfortable in our world. Growing children sometimes feel the need to go through stages of wide swings in first one direction and then the other. If given an atmosphere of acceptance, not pushed or prodded, they usually finally settle down to a comfortable combination of sociability and independence. They can take people or leave them alone. They feel free to express their feelings and opinions in a gentle, cool manner at the appropriate time and place.

In addition to not urging everyone to become overboard extroverts, this chapter also does not urge everyone to go about in a constant state of intimate "confession," a practice promoted in recent years by certain branches of the psychotherapeutic world, both amateur and professional, which might be termed the "let it all hang out school." They seem unaware that segments of the psyche which are pushed into public view in order to "hang out" often get chopped down or lopped off and left bruised and bleeding.

A high degree of vulnerability can be handled only by that small percentage of very secure human beings whose egos are so well integrated, whose self-esteem is so inviolable that nothing can arouse their anxiety. Very few people fall into this category. The "let it all hang out" school ignores the truth that the confessional, outside of professional confidentiality, is the stuff used in prison camps to murder and shatter sanity. Most people cannot stand being stripped naked. They should consider the prospect seriously before allowing it to happen, no matter what pressures are brought to bear.

In so-called "personality development" groups, often each individual is pushed into behavior he would not ordinarily choose for himself. The group's argument usually falls along the lines that such behavior is "open and honest" or "mature" or "uninhibited" or "growth producing." In truth, a really authentic person elects his own behavior, quite apart from peer or group pressure. To confront or challenge the group might reveal more honest feelings and mature independence than to go along with it. And that person may be more "open" and "uninhibited" if he admits to the group that he believes most of their proposed confessions and other "freeing" activities are nonsense.

Learning to express oneself need not be traumatic or threatening. The skill develops with practice and leads to that self-awareness referred to in an old unidentified Greek manuscript which reads:

The kingdom of heaven is within you,
and whosoever knoweth himself
shall find it there.

6.

The Magic of Relaxation and the Directed Daydream

Many persons are made tense and nervous by troubles which they cannot overcome. They don't know how to relax physically or mentally, and they don't know how to limber up their imagination and creativity in order to set goals and find solutions for their problems. Just telling them to relax and use their imaginations doesn't accomplish anything. They need a definite regime, a routine to be followed methodically.

A meditative technique called the "directed daydream"[8] teaches relaxation which soothes away tensions, elevates consciousness, and awakens the creative centers; it can also be used to help define goals and solve problems.

Relaxing and fantasizing are very natural processes. Children are born knowing the skills, they never have to be taught, but the Puritan ethic has stifled this natural, therapeutic urge. Over and over again parents admonish their children, "Stop daydreaming and do something useful!" According to Robert Ornstein, in his *Psychology of Consciousness*,[9] the banning of this exercise of the imagination is extremely unfortunate, if not absolutely harmful. He claims that a whole area of our brain is left to "die," in a manner of speaking. Instead of forbidding daydreaming, we ought to encourage it as a wellspring of creativity and inspiration.

Daydreaming has been purged not only by parents but by our very way of life which glorifies the extroverted activities. Solitude and quiet are needed for effective daydreaming, but for some sad, unfortunate reason, a child is believed to be sick or antagonistic if he wants to be alone. Everyone has forgotten that throughout history most of the greatest thinkers and greatest humanitarians have not been the back-slapping party-going types, but have been somewhat introverted, looking within themselves for their inspiration. They could not have become themselves had they allowed themselves to be caught up in the kind of impingement of the outer world which most people tolerate today: constant telephone conversations, TV programs, radio music, club meetings, kaffee-klatsches, sensitivity groups, cocktail parties, gymnasium classes, spectator sports, golf games, and heaven-knows-what. In our modern social setting, most persons are not alone for even five minutes a day. As the poet Wordsworth so aptly phrased it, "The world is too much with us."

A few unusual persons are inspired by working in a group, but for most really creative people, inspiration comes from within. Some time ago Benito Reyes, former philosophy professor of the University of the Philippines, holder of two Ph.D. degrees, lectured to a group in a local university. Despite his own extensive education, he beseeched his listeners, "Look within; there you'll find the deepest, truest answers, there you'll find the clues to fulfillment and harmony. Not in books, not in other people, but within yourself." As the author of *Applied Imagination* reminds us,[10]

Henry James made much of the "deep well of unconscious cerebration." Emerson took time out each day for "meditation quietly before brooks." Shakespeare called . . . (meditation) "the spell in which imagination bodies forth the forms of things unknown." Somerset Maugham wrote, "Reverie is the groundwork of creative imagination."

The directed daydream, which could also be termed "inner-imagery," is designed to help you look within. Of course it has been in use for hundreds of years, in one form or another, not only by children, but by adults all over the world. Certain types of prayer and meditation are directed daydream. We concentrate upon our desires, fantasizing their fulfillment. Also, as with the modern psychological techniques, we often relax our bodies and quiet our minds, then focus upon some object, perhaps a work of art, which has suggestive, creative effects.

Early in this century, the eminent Italian psychiatrist Roberto Assagioli, influenced by the innovative Hanscarl Leuner, incorporated this form of picturization meditation into his own system of psychology, Psychosynthesis.[11] Founded in Rome in 1926, this system propounds the notion that at the core of each individual is a Self that can direct the harmonious development of all aspects of personality, and "inner imagery" helps to reach that Self. This visualization is only one of many techniques set forth by Assagioli, but it is significant, because its use stresses, for the first time in the behavioral sciences, the need to stimulate the patient's imagination, creativity, and intuition in the therapeutic process.

Other European countries were quick to adopt Assagioli's directed daydream, especially France and Germany. However, the scientific minded United States was slower to see value in a psychotherapy which transcended reason and was not subject to statistical evaluation or behavioral modification observation. Finally, in 1957, the Psychosynthesis Research Foundation was incorporated in the United States, and its humanistic approach quickly took fire, for it now suited the temper of the times. The profession and the public were ready for such methods as meditation and picturization for reaching down to the Self and controlling the psyche. Jung, with his view of the collective unconscious, had now come into his own; and mystical Eastern religions, which heightened consciousness by means of meditation, had become widespread in America.

The power and effectiveness of the directed daydream was so quickly demonstrated that innumerable "courses" or "schools" sprang up all over the United States, each one claiming esoteric methods for utilizing arcane powers of the mind. Usually the founder of the school or course alleged that he alone had discovered the method, but of course, in each case he had merely superimposed some gimmick onto a method which was probably old when the Bible was written.

Inner imagery bears out the old Buddhist saying, "Where our thoughts go, there go the energies also." The more we concentrate on a goal in a relaxed, trusting way, the more our whole being strives toward it and usually attains it. As Rollo May phrases it,[12] "The wish is the beginning of orienting ourselves to the future." Successful inventors,[13] musicians, engineers, artists and many other people achieve certain goals or solve problems by augmenting their skill and effort with productive daydreaming. Steadily in their mind's eye is the goal they wish to achieve. Most of them feel drawn along by some unexplainable superior intelligence which works out the details for bringing about success. Many people ordinarily solve problems by visualizing them before going to sleep, calling upon a wiser self within to work out the solution; often the answer flashes into the mind immediately upon waking. Or often it seems that the superior intelligence proceeds to arrange events so that goals are attained or problems answered in a round about way. Many famous people have felt the presence of a "guide." Socrates spoke of his "daimon" who never erred, who always dictated the correct action or pathway; Robert Louis Stevenson spoke of his "Brownies" as helpers who worked for him while he slept.

The directed daydream not only stimulates creativity and intuition and facilitates "centering," but the same picturization, through the use of symbolism, helps to bring the psyche into harmony by satisfying deep-seated needs.[14] Most of these dream routines are playful and childlike, freeing the spontaneous child which lives within each of us.

An extremely important aspect of the directed daydream is complete relaxation, both physical and mental. Many "how-to" books and courses which teach some version of this type of meditative concentration neglect to lay stress on this imperative. The subject should feel a complete state of "letting go," so that there is no anxiety or tension of any kind.

The skills of relaxing and imaging interact in a harmonious symbiosis. The relaxation is needed for effective imaging, while the imaging is effective in prolonging the relaxation, itself an important factor in our organismic well-being.

Psychophysiologists have long ago become convinced that tension is the arch enemy of good health, that most diseases are psychosomatic,[15] induced by man's inability to handle the stresses of this demanding, complicated world.

When a person is threatened, physically or emotionally, when he feels frustrated, rejected, hurt, or fearful, the mind sends quick emergency messages so that the whole body's defense mechanism flares into action. This action was designed by Nature several million years ago to protect the organism, to provide ammunition for either "flight" or "fight" on those occasions when either behavior was needed, probably only rarely in those days.

But now the same defense mechanism is in constant boil of activity. Man's consciousness has been raised to a high sensitivity level and his mind has expanded so that his memory is longer and his imagination projects into the future. He has developed "civilized" guilts which eat at him. In addition he has fears about his own worth and ability to survive, memories of humiliations and rejections, worries and angers which can't be put aside. His environment and life-style keep him in a turmoil, sending almost a constant flow of anxiety messages to his brain.

On the way to work each morning, fighting commuter traffic, worrying about his bills, his job, his family, his self-image, his old age retirement, a man may send 500 such messages in the first hour of the day. His stream of consciousness is often a continuous gush of frustration: "I hope there's no cop around to see me squeeze through this signal turning red; one more ticket and up goes my insurance, even though the two accidents weren't really my fault, but all those insurance companies think about is the premium money; when you need them to pay up, they weasel out of it somehow. Oops, I'm almost out of gas; the boss'll really blow up if I stop at a station and show up late; I wonder if I'll make it; I'd hate to run out on this freeway, miles from anything, long walk. Yeh, but I'm supposed to walk more than I do; the doc told me just the other day the ticker isn't doing too well and I'll have an attack for sure if I don't get some of this belly off. Guess I'll have to slow down on the drinks before dinner; and Martha's hitting the bottle too much, really showed it the other night at the Finkles. Embarrassing as the devil. Got too friendly with old Ed. Wonder if my son Joe is getting into the liquor supply; seems to me it's disappearing awful fast lately. Never know what that kid's up to next. First the drugs; not sure he's out of that either. Wonder how I'm gonna save enough ahead to get those three young ones through college. It's Martha's fault we had them so close together, I wanted to wait a while. These days a kid's nowhere without that sheepskin. For that matter, I ought to have finished out at Tech before I got married. Never really sure of my job, keep promoting other guys ahead of me just because they got that piece of paper, most of them the smart-aleck type." And on and on and on.

The constant barrage of anxiety keeps the defense mechanism turning out a steady supply of several types of ammunition, which now in its overabundance no more defends the body than does a crazed rabid dog which turns on its own master. Instead, the ammunition tears at the body itself. The result is disease, perhaps eventually death.

Relaxation counteracts the anxiety messages, quiets the mental stampede, allows the body to function smoothly, easily, normally, as it was meant to. Most people find that the routine practice of relaxation night and morning, more if there is time, produces many unexpected benefits in their lives. The directed daydream always begins with some form of relaxation.

The daydream can be directed by the subject, by a therapist, or by tape recording. If the dream is directed by the subject himself, it additionally builds the concentration skill. However, for some people this takes practice. While directing his own inner imaging in a relaxed state, the subject is likely either to drift off to sleep, or to allow the mind to wander to undirected material, or to visualize dire outcomes of his problems, thereby reinforcing such outcomes. The tape recording is the best choice until the subject learns to concentrate. He should record his routine for himself, inasmuch as his own voice is the most influential and effective for this purpose.

Not every counselor directs the daydream exactly the same way, but I will give you my own method, which I have found to be very productive. The three routines given here in detail are basic and should be the most usable; they contain the most important symbols. The others all serve a number of different purposes, depending upon the actions and the symbols involved. As the dream is recounted, the subject both sees himself objectively and projects himself into the dream so that he experiences the dream through all the senses. It is important that he involve as many senses as possible.

Some subjects try to say that they don't visualize. This is nonsense. Without visualization we wouldn't understand words. What these people probably mean is that they don't visualize voluntarily any details which the narrator doesn't mention. They don't have the imagination to fill in the many "spaces," which the narrator must necessarily leave. Lacking this skill is unfortunate but only goes to point up the subject's great need for the development of imagination.

The directed daydream begins with the physical relaxation. Many articles have been written about the art of relaxing, but in case you've never had occasion to read one or have forgotten what they say, I'll give you a brief review.

The subject should lie supine without any part of his clothing binding or pressing on his body. If not wearing loose night clothes, he should loosen belts, remove shoes, and so on. He should remove eye glasses. If there is unavoidable noise, such as TV or street noise, he can tune a radio to very soft, nondisruptive music. The room should be dark, or semidark. Unless he falls asleep too easily, the subject should close his eyes.

He begins by taking about six slow, regular, deep breaths, breathing in slowly, holding the breath for an instant, then releasing the breath, then waiting an instant before repeating. Most people count at the rate of about one per second, so the breathing will be regular. For most persons a count of six for each inspiration and expiration with a count of two in between is about right. The details are not important. Each person should adjust the breathing to what's most comfortable for him.

After six breaths, the subject begins the actual relaxation, beginning with the top of the head. It's important to begin here. He gives attention ("concentrate" suggests tension), to each part of his body, relaxing the muscles in turn. He aims for a "rag doll" feeling, imaging each particular muscle to be relaxed and "let go." Beginning with the top of the head, he thinks to himself, "Top of the head, relax; around the mouth and chin, let go, relax. Muscles of the throat and neck, loose, let go. The shoulders and upper arms, relax. The lower arms, hands, fingers, loose, relax. Buttocks relax, let go. Thighs, let go. Muscles of the calves, feet and toes, relax, let go." Now, without breaking the pace, he returns to the head, thinking, "Forehead, eyes, around the nose, relaxed, loose. Around the mouth and chin, let go. relax." Now the subject is completely relaxed. If the therapist should pick up an arm or a leg, it would fall limply.

It is important to begin and end with the head, because many people wear what amounts to an iron mask, and the relaxation of the muscles of the face sets the stance for the whole body. It's very difficult to tense the rest of the body if the face is relaxed. Once a person has learned how to relax completely, he can remind himself several times a day to relax and his body will respond instantly. It is a very restful practice, for much of our tiredness comes from the unnecessary tenseness of our bodies.

Next, the subject decelerates brain wave activity by the

countdown procedure. Scientists claim that during ordinary activity, the brain is operating at the "Beta" level, but the slower "Alpha" level is more conducive to the creative and intuitive process. Biofeedback research proves that it is not difficult to slow the brain rhythm down to seven to ten-and-a-half cycles per second instead of the usual rhythm of fourteen to twenty-eight cycles per second. Relaxation and the desire to do so bring about the shift rather easily.

In order to accomplish this deceleration, the subject, still keeping relaxed, languidly counts down from ten to one, feeling himself growing more and more mentally detached and lazy as he does so. He can visualize himself in an elevator, drifting down from the tenth story of a building, or picture himself riding in a balloon which floats to earth more and more slowly. "Ten, slow, down; nine, slow, down; eight, slow, down; seven, slow, down; six, slow, down; five, slow, down; four, slow, down; three, slow, down; two, slow, down; one, down.

Now, still relaxed and comfortable, the subject is ready for his daydream, directed either by the therapist, a tape recording, or himself. Remember, the subject involves all the senses so that the experience is as complete as possible, and his imagination fills in any details not furnished by the narration.

You are alone in a garden, a wild garden, near a bubbling stream. You hearing the gurgling sounds of the water as it splashes over stones of all colors. The little river has a sandy bank, but you are standing in plush-like green grass. It's a mildly warm day; you feel the pleasant sun on your arms and legs as the bright white light floods down over you. Then a soft breeze stirs the pine trees in the distance. You feel the little breeze and smell the pine scent which is carried by the breeze and you hear the gentle rushing sound, as the branches sway slightly. You hear a sound beside you and then see that a deer with large velvety antlers has come from among the trees, on his way to the stream. This is a magic garden, so of course the buck is not afraid of you. Rather, he comes up to you, curious about this new visitor, stretching out his head toward you, to inquire and sniff. As you pet him, you feel the sleekness of his neck and then the velvet of his antlers. His curiosity satisfied, he goes on his way for a drink. You hear a birdsong and finally locate the brightly colored bird, perched on a low shrub near the river. The singing continues as you approach. You feel that the bird would hop onto your finger if you so desired. You are filled with peace at the beauty and harmony of the day. You deeply inhale the fragrance of a wild rose and finally locate it blooming not far from you, the pink blossoms in a wild profusion. Just then from beneath the bush hops a small brown rabbit. He, too, is curious about your intrusion, but he is not afraid. He hops closer, stands up and sniffs curiously as you pet his fur and scratch behind his ears. Finally, he hops away, nibbling at the grass here and there. Now you see some purple iris and other brightly colored flowers growing in clumps among the green grass. You look deep to the centers of several flowers. You walk toward the river, deciding to go wading. You slip off your sandals and feel the warm sand on your feet. Stepping into the cool water is refreshing, so you wade along towards the sounds of rushing water, evidently caused by a waterfall somewhere ahead. At this time a doe and her fawn come to the stream and you go toward the bank to meet them. They too are friendly and curious. You pet the little speckled fawn, and he is so excited by this attention that he dances away, bouncy and stiff-legged. Traveling in a little circle, he finally returns to his mother's side. His mother watches, attentive but not concerned. Nearby a little squirrel is not so happy. Afraid you will find his winter's cache, he sits up and chatters bossily at you, his tail twitching to reinforce his words. He darts this way and that, finally dashing into his home in the ground. You walk along the water's edge, still hearing the sound of the waterfall ahead of you. As you round the bend you see the water gushing out of the rocks above. At the base is a large, quiet pool. You cannot resist the temptation to slip out of your clothes and dive into the pool, enjoying the fresh fragrance of the water and its silkiness against your body. You dip and splash and twist and turn, all of which attracts an otter who watches from the bank. Finally, deciding he likes your games, he enters the pool and plays tag with you, at times nudging you from behind, only to dash away before you can catch him. Finally, the game tires you and you make for the shore. As you dry yourself, on the towel which has magically appeared, you watch the pounding of the waterfall, feeling its power and enjoying the rainbows created by the mist which flies around it. A bright butterfly circles around you, as if wondering about this strange flower, and you hear the buzzing of a bee as it enters one of the iris. The sun is higher now and you are feeling lazy. You slip into your clothes and stretch out in the sweet-smelling grass. Lying on your back, you watch the puffy white clouds floating over your head. Ever so slowly they drift, giving you the feeling that you too are drifting. As you watch the clouds against the sapphire sky, they gradually change shape: now a ship with billowy sails, now an angel with large white wings. You grow drowsier and drowsier, as the sounds around you seem to recede into the distance. Soon you are asleep.

After once going through this basic daydream, the subject can subsequently tailor the dream to yield the greatest dividend of pleasure and relaxation. If the daydream is tape recorded, of course the recording must be planned and narrated ahead of time. But if the meditation is directed spontaneously by the subject, it can be recreated each time, according to his mood and whim, thereby giving his imagination more exercise. In this nature scene he should make certain always to include the water. It would be well not to place the forest too close, nor to include animals which are likely to arouse fear. Remember to concentrate on all the senses. If anything in the dream is the least bit disturbing, leave it out next time. This is usually a very pacifying fantasy for persons who are emotionally upset.

The next daydream is a most important one for problem solving. The subject goes through the same relaxing and countdown. After that he meditates on a short version of the garden dream. Then, instead of going to sleep in the dream, he continues:

You decide to climb to the top of the waterfall, going along an easy path beside the fall which winds in such a way that the walk seems no effort at all. As you rise above the lower area, you look across at a range of snowy mountains, and feel their great tranquility as you walk. Finally, at the top of the falls, where the water gushes out of the rock, you look to the right and see a castle. You recognize at once that this is your home, beautiful and well kept. As you cross the courtyard, you come to the entry, where lazy trees are in blossom and a lush garden flourishes. The large door opens easily, and when you enter the hallway, you see a winding staircase leading to the next floor. From the hallway, you can see the doors to the rooms above and know that the room you seek is on the right. You mount the stairs, and again the door pushes open easily, revealing a beautiful room, a study wonderfully equipped. The room is of the colors and furnishings most pleasing to you. You stand and take in every detail: the bookcases, the rich carpeting, the handsome furnishings. There is a fire in the fireplace, and facing it is a table with several comfortable chairs. The room is also equipped with a telephone, a radio, a small computer, and a TV set all designed to function in a unique way. It has anything else you would like to have in a pleasant work room where you go to plan and arrange your life. You step to one of the casement windows and open it outward, letting in the fresh air as you look down at the countryside around you and across to the range of snow-capped mountains. In the distance you spot a church on a knoll and hear its chimes. For a moment you gaze at the church, admiring the spires and imagining its stained glass windows and peaceful interior. Turning back to the room, you turn on the very special TV and then sit very relaxed in a comfortable chair to watch for a few moments. You consciously control the TV program with your mind, flashing on the screen the way you want different aspects of your life to develop. You fantasize exact details and seem to live the events depicted. Whatever you are most interested in at the moment appears on the screen the way you would like it to materialize: your family life, or your career, or the travels you would like to take, or anything else you are looking forward to. You focus for a long time on this, the pictures you most desire to see in your life, visualizing each scene according to your wishes. Perhaps you use the telephone to call someone you would like to talk with, perhaps someone who can give you the answer to questions, or someone with whom you would like to improve relations. You straighten out your difficulties. Perhaps you use the computer to pose a question or state a problem. You will drop the question into the computer on a card which also states that the answer can be sent to you later, after the solution has been carefully worked out. As you release the card into the computer you think, "Let it go, just let it go! It will be taken care of." You use any of the equipment in your study as your resourcefulness dictates. Now you hear a knock at the door. Before you answer it, you know that although you've never seen him (or her) before, this is a devoted friend and mentor, who will always come when you need him, as counselor, teacher, problem solver or companion. You answer the door and see the person in the doorway. He (or she) introduces himself, you embrace, and seat yourselves in front of the fire. You talk of your life and what you're striving towards. Your mentor assures you that he will always help you, as long as you live. Finally, after sharing with him your aims, goals, ideas, opinions and problems, you both rise and say goodbye, promising to meet tomorrow. Later, you close up your study, descend the stairs, and walk into the garden, feeling peaceful and confident.

A few words about this directed daydream, the basics of which ought to be followed rather closely, so as to include all the important elements. Of course, the subject furnishes the room as he pleases and varies the routine of problem solving according to his own creative imagination, suiting the inner imagery to his own purposes, as with all directed daydreams. There are endless bits of equipment or routines he might use to visualize his goals and state his problems. Except for modern machinery, such as the TV and computer, which encompasses the ideas of speed, power, and efficiency, the symbols involved are very old. For instance, the nature symbols date back to the very creation of man, whereas the castle is depicted in Spenser's *Faery Queen*. If the subject doesn't feel comfortable with a castle as his home, he may certainly redesign any kind of dwelling which suits his fancy.

Of course I hope no one is naive enough to believe that goals are reached by merely daydreaming. As Rollo May explains, "The will gives maturity to the wish."[16] Effort and skill are always one's most important tools for building the good life and fulfilling dreams.

The third daydream is independent of the other two. It's a very "freeing" fantasy:

You are walking along the beach on a mild, sunny day. You are practically alone. In places just off shore there are large rocks which cause the waves to crash and then with a booming sound, rebound and spray high into the air. But in other places, the waves come in steadily, gathering force and height, faster and faster, churning forward into a high, thin sheet which curls and finally collapses with a roar, only to recede. Wave after wave follow one another in this game. You smell the salt air and watch the waves perform this everlasting attack on the shore. You feel the great power and beauty as you walk along, the damp sand crunching under your bare feet. Now and then you bend down to pick up a particularly beautiful seashell. You admire its pearly surfaces, feel its smoothness, and put it to your ear to hear the "roaring of the sea." At times you kick at a clump of seaweed which has been rejected by the ocean, now partly dry and crusted with sand. A small puppy bounds along, coming, it seems, from nowhere. He rushes up with great wriggles of happiness. You pick up a stick of driftwood and toss it ahead of you. The puppy goes leaping after it, and returns in a proud, pattering trot, the stick awkward in his mouth, almost too big for him to handle. You laugh and grab at the stick, engaging in a tug-of-war before the puppy gives up his prize. Then he stands barking expectantly in front of you. The two of you repeat this game several times; sometimes you throw the stick into the shallow water and the puppy hesitates a moment before defying the threat of the giant waves beyond. Suddenly the puppy is attracted to someone behind you and darts away. The puppy has put you into a playful mood. You run and take a giant leap into the air, like a ballet dancer. Again you run and leap; and yet a third time. Then you turn a cartwheel, and after a few steps turn another. Next you dance and skip and swing your body in wide free movements which express your joy. You get closer and closer to the water's edge so that the little waves grab at you and splash you. Then you run in a great burst of speed until finally, exhausted, you throw yourself onto the sand. Reclining there you watch the blue sky and the seagulls out at sea, wheeling and soaring. You hear their shrill cries as they, from time to time, dive for food and quarrel over the choicest morsels. You watch the shore birds, walking jerkily and stiff-legged as they peck here and there for insects. Finally, you get to your feet and again begin walking. Over the sounds of the ocean and the birds, you hear the music of a calliope ahead. You remember there's a boardwalk and a merry-go-round not far away, so you lose no time, but walk at a brisk pace. Now you see the crowds of people on the boardwalk and at the carousel, the bright horses as they go 'round and 'round, their lavish decoration all sparkle and gilt. You choose the proudest looking red horse. As the music continues its piping and crashing, the merry-go-round slowly pulls into motion, gradually increasing its pace until you feel you are flying, as the horse rhythmically gallops around his festive arena. Each time you approach the arm holding the rings, you lean far out, grabbing and hoping yours is the brass one. Many times you are disappointed, but still enjoy the fun of flipping the silver ring into the pasteboard clown's broad mouth. Eventually the great thing happens. The brass ring is next! Laughing, you grab it and clutch it tightly, slipping it over two fingers for safe keeping. Much too soon the pace slows. You realize rather sadly that the ride is over and slide down the side of your beloved prancing steed, then step down from the carousel. The brave, brash music of the calliope continues. You smell the unmistakable fragrance of cotton candy, and find not too far away the man who sells it. You hold the large cornucopia lightly, trying to lick or bite the chunks of pink sugary sweetness without smearing your face. But it seems to reach out to you and you soon realize the stickiness cannot be avoided. You drop the last of the candy into the trashcan, splash the drinking fountain water onto your face and walk past the smells of hot dogs and popcorn toward the roller coaster ticket office. Already you can hear the screams and shouts of those riding this great monster of thrills, but with combined excitement and fear you buy your ticket and climb into the front car. The ride is exactly what you remembered. Almost too fearful and exciting to bear, as the car slowly chugs uphill and then in a torrent of speed plummets down the other side. Others around you are screaming, but you close your eyes and clench your teeth tightly, hanging on for fear you'll fly out of the car to be crushed far below. The sensations gather and you feel you too will laugh and scream all at the same time. Finally after many climbs and drops, the car slows and the ride is ended. Grateful to be on solid ground, but still excited, you go out the gate and mingle again with the crowd. Now you make your way back along the ocean front. The sun is beginning to set and colors both sky and water a faint pink. The ocean seems quieter. Your mood is peaceful. You look at the brass ring in your hand and smile.

Again, the subject may vary this directed daydream to encompass anything which is spontaneous and free; or he can delete anything which makes him tense or unhappy. He ought not to leave out the ocean, the free dancing movements, the puppy, and the carousel, including the brass ring.

In addition, I will list some other possible fantasies. Anyone can elaborate on them according to his mood and taste. Of course the subject's imagination will fill in myriad details.

1. You are on a quiet tropical island. In the distance you hear a rumbling, and feel the earth tremble somewhat. Then you witness the eruption of a volcano. You build up the action gradually. You are not threatened, not afraid. You are simply fascinated by the violent action and enjoy the feeling of catharsis it evokes.

2. You fish a quiet stream. Picture each detail of preparation, baiting the hook, casting, etc. Finally catch the fish, take it from the hook. Repeat.

3. You watch a rosebush grow from a small bush to a larger one. Then watch a small green bud appear, the sepals separate, the bud grows larger, and finally you see a spot of color at the tip. Then watch the rose as it ever so slowly comes to full bloom. Smell the fragrance. Feel the velvet petals. Now introject yourself. You *are* this rose.

4. You do a daydream in slow motion. You're in a lupine studded meadow. In slow motion, hair flying, you dance, leap, turn, kick your heels. You laugh and let yourself go. Still in slow motion you go to a small hilltop and then lie down and roll to the bottom, over and over in a mass of buttercups, absorbing the yellowness. Then you run through a field of tall grass, still in slow motion, with the green all around you.

5. You are a wild duck, migrating with the flock. You look down on all manner of scenery as you fly, then float on a pond and watch the sunset.

6. You relive all the peak experiences in your life, those moments which were the most beautiful, happy, or thrilling. Begin from the time you were very small.

7. You become a bird, any kind you choose, which is flying through a mythological rainbow which you can be aware of while you are in

it. Feel the effect of each color, the fragrances it produces, etc. Perhaps, the red would make you feel physically healthy, the orange make you aware of your strength, the yellow seem to clear your mental faculties, the green make you feel healed and refreshed, the blue make you aware of the goodness in the world—yours and everyone's—the violet make you aware of your will power.

One's own imagination can create any narration he wants, but the suggested daydreams take into account vital symbols. Repeat, one ought always leave off any fantasies which are upsetting in any way.

Some final words: Dr. Assagioli warns that people who are at all inclined to hear voices from within, or to have any other untoward reaction ought to discontinue the fantasizing entirely. Instead, their total energy ought to be turned outward, toward the world, rather than inward. Of course, no one should spend overmuch of his time in fantasizing when leading an average day-to-day life. Pulling too much into one's own world is an unhealthy escape. Many people who find this regime efficacious spend as much as an hour a day, sometimes in two half-hour sessions, but no more than that. Some spend no more than fifteen minutes. The directed daydreams, especially the first basic one, is often used by counselors simply as a treatment of the moment to quiet and center a person who feels distraught. If the counselee finds the routine beneficial, he can continue it each day at home. After the initial explanation and directions, the counselor needs to spend no more office time on the routine.

Even if the subject has no interest in a complicated directed daydream, the relaxation exercises followed by a few minutes' meditation centered upon some pleasing mental picture usually are found to be restful and soothing. Anyone who practices this simple routine daily will reap some benefit. The physical, mental, and emotional are so closely tied that physical and mental quietude help to relieve emotional tension.

Counselors who are in tune with humanistic psychology often find the directed daydream their most effective tool and can refer to many case histories. Cooperative clients, willing to adopt a methodical daily routine report results which sound like modern day miracles.

I am reminded of Susan, who came to me because, as she explained it, "In the past year I often have days when I really feel as though I'm going to pieces. The anxiety builds up until I can't stand it. If I were on drugs, I'd wonder if I were having a bad trip. I've been to my doctor and to a psychiatrist. They both tell me just to calm down; there's nothing wrong with me, there's nothing to worry about."

Susan's history showed that she'd been through a divorce and for a time had tried to work at two jobs in order to clear up some debts and support her little girl. At first she'd attributed the "nervous spells" to fatigue so had quit one job. But despite the more relaxed schedule, the attacks of anxiety and agitation had continued. Susan had been reared by a puritanical mother who believed that daydreaming was a sinful waste of time and had often admonished Susan, "Don't let your imagination run away with you!" Therefore, obedient Susan had always been careful not to let her mind wander into fantasy for fear her mental processes would go completely out of control. Instead, whenever she had time on her hands, she forced herself to think of some mental exercise, such as rehearsing her times tables or conjugating irregular French verbs.

At first Susan was reluctant to let herself fantasize; her childhood conditioning was too strong. But finally, as her trust grew, she found she enjoyed the relaxing experience and practiced it daily. Inasmuch as she was lonely for male companionship, whenever she visualized her future life, she included an attactive man, a blue-eyed, Nordic, outdoor type, who would be devoted to both her and her child. At first she giggled a lot about this part of her daydream, but eventually, when the man actually appeared, with exactly the cultural background and personality she'd fantasized she was sobered as well as astounded. Susan's anxiety attacks grew less and less frequent and finally disappeared. Fortunately, the man is still with her.

Another client was a space engineer who came to me along with his wife for marriage counseling. As it turned out, their problems were minimal, but nevertheless I asked, as is my custom, that each spouse come for a few sessions alone. Then they would continue jointly. Actually, there was no obvious reason for me to mention the "inner imagery" to this man, but my intuition prompted me to introduce the whole concept. Normally, I am very circumspect about suggesting it; although meditation is an acceptable idea to many people, some clients would lose confidence in a counselor who suggested such radical, mystical ideas. In his case, the results were electrifying. Within the week he could solve engineering problems with no more than a few minutes' meditation while relaxed on a sofa in his office. In the beginning when I first narrated a directed daydream and gave him the instructions, I warned that problem solving usually took many hours, sometimes longer. But he soon discovered that if any solution were possible, he could demand that answer to be delivered within a few minutes. So almost overnight his whole career advanced strikingly, while his work load actually lessened.

Another case which comes to mind is not a client of mine; I heard of him through another counselor who practices this theory. The client is a general contractor who now rises each morning about an hour earlier than previously. After his relaxation routine, he envisions the remainder of the day, step by step, as he would like it to go. He claims that usually the building business is fraught with frustration and even defeat. Much time spent on figuring bids is completely wasted, with no remuneration; subcontractors who must be depended upon to complete their particular work specialty before the job can go forward often fail to appear, week after week; specified materials are not delivered as promised, or, even worse, become unavailable; labor crews are often unreliable and unpredictable; bad weather or theft of building materials can halt a job completely. At one time he'd threatened to go into another line of work in order to preserve his sanity. But now all that has changed. By devoting an hour each morning to relaxation and inner imagery, most days go smoothly with scarcely any of the irritating situations he had experienced in the past. As a sidelight, I feel compelled to mention that just about everyone who knows this man asks him where he discovered the fountain of youth. They are puzzled by his apparent reversal of the aging process!

These examples are, of course, outstanding; but everyone I've known to follow faithfully the routines of relaxation and directed daydream invariably comments upon new feelings of peace, security, and direction never before experienced. They've found, as expressed in Proverbs, "As a man thinketh in his heart, so is he."

7.

Some Notes on Personality Structure

You've already learned, one way or another, a great deal of personality theory. In the present day world Freud and Berne are common nouns and small children talk to their dolls about "complexes and hang-ups." Sometimes it seems that just about everyone, young and old, is playing psychologist. *

Only recently has behavioral science been regarded as a separate discipline, but serious thinkers have always recognized certain psychological principles. Ancient religious leaders, poets, and historians have all observed the workings of the human mind and emotions. They have known the destructive effect of pride, greed and jealousy, and the power of love and courage. They could predict the triumph of the wise, courageous hero or the failure of the rash, impulsive youth.

But until the late nineteenth century, no one attempted to delve into the anatomy and physiology of the psyche in such a way as to examine both its outward and inward aspects, its sources of energy, its patterns of development, and its responses to environmental influences. In the past hundred years psychological theory has come to resemble a huge oak, developing from the trunk into many limbs, in some places ensnared, in some places showing signs of dead wood, in some places vital and flourishing. Certain branches are especially useful for understanding the mental-emotional self.

One of these is Alfred Adler's theory that the most important psychological drive is the need to overcome a sense of inferiority in order to feel secure, free of fears and anxieties. Supremacy over one's environment is attempted by compensating, in whatever way available, for the inferiority with which one is born. As Gardner Murphy paraphrases it,

> . . . Experience of life in the newborn child is one of weakness, inadequacy, and frustration. He finds strong, active people who go marching about; who decide what they want to do and do it. . . . He is a little helpless object . . . wanting to control . . . his activity . . . and liberate . . . himself from the domination of this big, inscrutable world. Power, in other words, is the first good, just as weakness is the first evil; and compensation becomes simply a name for the struggle of the individual in the direction of power. . . . The child develops, as a rule, a rather consistent and workable method of compensating—a method depending upon . . . the personalities of his parents . . . later the nature of neighborhood and community pressure determines what it takes to get over being a helpless little baby. . . . Individual personality takes shape as a device for coping with the frustrations of infantile experience.[17]

Early in life the child thinks only of physical superiority, but as he grows older he realizes that to overcome a sense of inferiority he must feel worthwhile on several other levels— spiritual, social, and mental. The more civilized he is, the less emphasis he places on primitive physical strength. In other words, the dominating drive in life is the desire to feel powerful, important, worthy, successful, and intelligent. Deprived of these feelings of adequacy, a person of any age suffers a whole spectrum of anxieties; he is defensive, fear-ridden, and tense, even though he may do an excellent cover-up job that is compensatory in some way. Not only do the anxieties rob him of life's most soothing asset—peace of mind—the covering up often saps his energies. In addition, more complicated cover-ups appear as crippling neuroses, or even psychoses.

Most simply stated, this urgency for superiority is no more than the instinct of survival, the instinct which warns that in this fish-eat-fish sea of life, little fish must find ways to compensate in order to hold their own. *Potency* means *life, impotency* means *death.*

Animals use a wide variety of compensatory methods and it's both useful and amusing to note that each method has its counterpart, on either a literal or figurative level, in the human social structure. In addition to a show of actual physical strength, animals may emit loud noises to appear important or ferocious and they may exhibit quick, threatening tempers. They may sting, bite, puff up, run away, or pull into a protective shell. They may control others in a cat-and-mouse manner or more indirectly by arousing affection or pity, or appearing to be weak, perhaps simulating a broken wing or leg. Or animals may use craft or guile to outwit other creatures. Of course their most usual bid for power is to travel in herds or packs, each carefully conforming so he will be accepted and protected. Most animals depend upon only two or three types of compensation tricks, but if you've had Macaque monkeys as pets, you know that they, like homo sapiens, have mastered every one in this list!

You can easily match the list of animal defenses to behavior you've often seen in yourself and others, for everyone employs these compensatory devices to a greater or lesser degree, depending upon each person's basic sense of self-worth. Those who are unsure of themselves will need more frequent and stronger doses of compensatory soothing syrup; everyone needs at least an occasional sip.

From the most primitive times down to the present,

physical strength has been valued as a sign of superiority, a threat to those who are less able to defend themselves. Old myths emphasize the virility of their heroes, men able to strangle a lion or slay a dragon or survive hand-to-hand combat, and all small boys, probably beginning with Cain and Abel, quickly learn to display their muscles and to brag about their physical prowess. Athletic meets draw large crowds for displays of all kinds of physical skill, to the delight and admiration of those who identify with sports heroes. At boxing matches no doubt each spectator, at some level of consciousness, sees himself as the mighty brute force lashing out at his enemy. If the public were really interested solely in boxing skill, as it sometimes maintains, the heavyweight championship would not always be the chief box office attraction. Everyone admires big men. Studies show that tall men are more often chosen for administrative positions, engender more confidence in every walk of life, and are generally more successful financially because they're offered more opportunities. Primitive man quickly learned to augment his feeling of strength with a club or rock, or, later a knife, and still later a gun.

Physical strength may be demonstrated not only on an athletic field but by an object a person identifies with, such as a car or motorcycle. It is no accident that car advertisements most often point out a car's speed and power, and that cyclists obviously enjoy revving up their motors and roaring forth with a burst of power that sounds like a jet takeoff; one of the fascinations of a machine is that its strength, sound, and speed surpass that of a mere mortal and give its owner a sense of potent superiority. No doubt the automobile has become the identity stamp of America. Its high cost, speed, and power can impress not only friends, neighbors, and relatives, but thousands of strangers on the highway as well. An aggressive driver can express his contempt and skill and therefore his own superiority in all kinds of dangerous traffic maneuvers.

It was mentioned that another on the list of animal compensation devices was noise. Whether it be made by a voice, musical instrument, or machine, a noise can serve to frighten, show disdain, drown out whatever threatens one, or just gain notice. A baby's cry is his first declaration of his existence, his first demand for recognition. Throughout life the voice remains an important factor of identity. The voices of those who need to overcome their sense of inferiority may be aggressively loud or beguilingly soft; in either case they may excite interest, as does the compulsive talker who cannot bear to lose the spotlight his voice commands. The talkative schoolchild, the telephone addict, the long-winded after-dinner speaker all share one common desire—to be important enough to possess another's attention.

Like animals, humans also may use anger as a weapon, figuratively stinging and biting in order to dominate others. Most often the quick-tempered man is one who is disappointed with his own self-image, who feels put down and rejected. Frustrated with his failure to command the recognition and respect he somehow expects, he tries to force this high regard by means of anger and threats of violence. This is equally true of groups which feel ignored or ostracized.

Humans also may "puff" themselves up in order to appear superior. They may brag, exaggerate their success in the retelling, pretend to "know it all," "play God," or be excessively "bossy." Eric Berne points out that neurotic persons seem unable to relate to others on an adult-to-adult level, that is, to treat others as rational, mature equals in a relaxed give-and-take cooperative manner. Either they must be the "parent," the authority who exercises his power over others; or they must be the "child," the manipulator who inveigles others to protect and support him. The animal world has its manipulators too, animals which make a show of affection or a pretense of helplessness, both of which are simply tools to aid survival.

As for running away, most wild creatures are quick to separate themselves from danger in the first moments of threat. Humans usually do the same—they run away from physical danger and also from those who make them feel threatened emotionally. For instance, young people often leave home because they cannot bear the constant reminder, inherent in family grouping, that they are in many ways inferior to their parents—younger, less experienced, less knowledgeable, less respected, less in control of their own lives. Children want to escape parents who, accustomed to exercising supremacy, find it almost impossible to address their children on an adult-to-adult level even if they really intend to do so. They assert their authority in a hundred little gestures or tones of voice or family habits. As soon as the offspring leave the nest, no longer supported economically and emotionally by parental authority, they are free to assume an adult role in their own good time and to define their own identity. In short, they usually grow up.

Of course there are many other ways of running away, of escaping the evidence of one's inferiority. A person may simply deny that such evidence exists, no matter how patent it may be to everyone else. You have met people who simply refuse to believe that they sing off-key or that behind the wheel of a car they are a traffic hazard. No one could possibly convince them of their inferiority in these skills. Other persons escape facing their inferiority by blaming their failures on other people or other conditions. They blame their parents who supposedly gave them a poor start in life, or a teacher who had "pets," or a boss who promoted only his personal friends, or a society which hasn't provided enough jobs for everyone. Their blaming and self-excusing extend endlessly. Others escape by means of drugs, alcohol, food, or incessant diverting entertainment, such as the excitement of gambling or sexual conquests or violent TV programs. Still others withdraw so completely into a fantasy world they are unable to return to reality.

This fantasy world may also be termed "protective shell." Other "shells" are elevated status, powerful authority, extreme wealth, superior learning, or great fame. Usually these shells are not as secure as they may seem from the exterior, but they are often sought after by those who feel threatened.

Failing all these efforts to establish a feeling of strength and worth, many persons resort to craft or cleverness, even to the point of operating outside the law. Outwitting the police and defying the whole social system pump up their feelings of superior intelligence and courage.

Most universal in its offer of support and security is acceptance by one's own clan, group, herd, pack, or class. Few people can endure a life without family, friends, or a feeling of "belonging" to one group or another. So important is the herd instinct and so influential is the group pressure that behavior which is frowned upon by the total group rarely exists. For example, the problems of alcoholism or high divorce rate simply don't exist in societies which absolutely abhor those practices. No matter how tempting it might be to get gloriously drunk or to abandon an ugly, old mate, the thought of becoming an outcast keeps almost everyone "walking the line."

Comparing the drives and motivations of humans to those of animals is not meant to suggest that mankind doesn't think much straighter than do the cows and pigs. It suggests rather that defenses are natural to all creatures, a necessary part of development, deeply ingrained devices of nature to aid all forms of life in the continuous process of adaptation and survival.

Only excessive use of these defenses indicates personality maladjustment. Like Sisyphus, condemned forever to push a heavy stone up a hill, those who suffer inferiority feelings must incessantly toil for security; therefore, their defenses are drudging along constantly. Ironically, some of these defenses are not in harmony with one another. Violence, bragging, withdrawing, and other antisocial acts often result in some form of group rejection, which just magnifies the original feeling of inferiority. Of course it must be realized that defenses are unconscious, or involuntary, or the object of rationalization. Few people, especially those with personality problems, understand the roots of their behavior.

If you shuffle through these many types of defenses, you will find they fall into two groups. As Adler recognized, in the effort to overcome a sense of inferiority, each person develops into one of two types.

The infant realizes at an early age that there are other human beings who are able to satisfy their urges more completely, and are better prepared to live. . . . In this way he learns to overvalue the size and stature which enable one to open a door, or the ability to move heavy objects, or the right of others to give commands and claim obedience to them. A desire to grow, to become as strong or even stronger than all others, arises in his soul. To dominate those who are gathered about him becomes his chief purpose in life, since his elders, though they act as if he were inferior, are obligated to him because of his very weakness. Two possibilities of action lie open to him. On the one hand, to continue activities and methods which he realizes the adults use, and on the other hand, to demonstrate his weakness, which is felt by these same adults as an inexorable demand for their help. We continually find this branching of psychic tendencies. . . . The formation of types begins at this early period. Whereas some children develop in the direction of the acquisition of power and the selection of a courageous technique which results in their recognition, others seem to speculate on their own weakness, and attempt to demonstrate it in the most varied forms. One need but recall the attitude, the expression, and the bearing of individual children to find individuals who fit into one group or the other.[18]

The first type can be classified as the independent, dominative type, and the second as the dependent, manipulative type.

On another page is a diagram which attempts to simplify my own adaptation of Adler's theory. You'll find that the chart is divided in half, the top half concerned with Tigers and the lower half with Pussycats. The Tigers are the independent, leadership type personalities, Adler's "acquisition of power and the selection of the a courageous technique" type. The Pussycats are the dependent, cooperative type of personalities, Adler's "speculate on their own weakness" type. Toward the center, where both these types are near the point of security and self-esteem, are the "O.K. Tigers" and the "O.K. Pussycats."

In short, each type can be "O.K." and comfortable with its individual method of operation if it has overcome most feelings of inferiority, if it feels worthy and strong. The independent type, the Tigers, we regard in our culture as having agential masculine traits. They usually strive toward positions of influence or leadership—executives, supervisors, administrators, or other leadership roles. The dependent types, the Pussycats, we regard in our culture as having communal, feminine traits. They usually strive toward positions involving human relations—sales persons, nurses, ministers, or other humanitarian vocations. Some professions would be sought by both, depending upon the attitude of the individual involved. A teacher could emphasize the pleasure of demonstrating his control over the class, or he could emphasize his humanitarian feelings about children. Of course a person's personality doesn't always suit his job. Also, some jobs have no particular personality type qualifications.

Toward the center of the chart, in the "O.K." areas, the personality characteristics are not very marked. A person who is secure doesn't have to show off his power, nor does he have to knock himself out showing how kind and helpful he can be. The more a person has overcome his feelings of inferiority, the more self-esteem he's built up, the less he needs to use defenses. He tends to be autonomous, confidently behaving in a free and spontaneous manner. He has a realistic self-image; neither overly modest nor overly proud; he accepts himself with good humor. He doesn't try to show off. He's "easy in the harness."

As the Tigers and Pussycats move farther away from the center line of security, they begin to show signs of being unhealthy, the "Sick Tigers" on one side, the "Sick Pussycats" on the other.

Sick Tigers are in bad humor and really "roar" and "bite!" Usually determined not to show any "soft" emotions or weakness of any kind, they attempt to dominate others by their display of power—threats, criticism, temper, loud noises, boasting, deploring, blaming, bossing. They must always be strong and "right" and in control of other people. They themselves can't stand any put-down. They often risk death on the highway rather than give way to another motorist. They may collect status symbols—money, power, position—just for the sake of demonstrating their superi-

ADLERIAN PERSONALITY CHART
INSTINCT FOR SURVIVAL
(Striving for feelings of self-worth, strength, security)
TYRANT
(Controls by power—may arouse fear in others)

"Top Dog" Personality Threatens (noise, words, etc.) Must be "right" Dominates, bosses, judges, criticizes (cuts down to size) Brags Gathers symbols of power (money, status, physical strength)	**SICK TIGER** Message: "See how powerful I am. You've *got* to respect me."
Governs Assumes responsibility Guides, leads Teaches Protects Nurtures	**O.K. TIGER** Message: "I am my own person. My natural bent is toward leadership."

H E A L T H Y   Z O N E   H E A L T H Y   Z O N E

Security

Nurtures Socializes skillfully Shows warmth Cooperates Is kind, thoughtful	**O.K. PUSSYCAT** Message: "I am my own person. My natural bent is toward cooperation."
Pleases people at all costs Is dependent. "Needs" people Whines—(sometimes emphasizes helplessness) "Kills with kindness" Self-sacrificing—"Doormat" personality.	**SICK PUSSYCAT** Message: "See how good and kind (and perhaps helpless) I am—you've *got* to love me."

MARTYR
(Controls by manipulation—may arouse pity or guilt in others)

ority. They demand respect and obedience. The extreme types, the tyrants (like Hitler), are the most gratified when they arouse abject fear.

"Sick Pussycats," at the other extreme, thirst for attention. They are usually underfoot, doormat personalities, rubbing against ankles and demanding protection. Extremely dependent, sometimes upon drugs, food, or alcohol, as well as upon people, they attempt to control people by arousing guilt, often using killing-with-kindness tactics so that everyone feels indebted. They seem to say, "Look how loving, kind, good, and hard-working I am, and all for you. I need you. You have to love me. If you don't I'll make you sorry!" Like Portnoy's mother, they beat their breasts and confess,

> You know what my biggest fault is? I hate to say it about myself, but I'm too good . . . and I get kicked in the teeth in return—and my fault is that as many times as I get slapped in the face, I can't stop being good.[19]

Most people feel powerless against these manipulators. There's no way to refuse their burdensome generosities, generosities for which they will demand heavy repayment. Sometimes that repayment must be in the most precious ingredient of life, time itself, for often these dependent personalities must feed upon personal attention. Declaring that they "love people," this type is apt to engage in endless monologues, often detailed and repetitive, impervious to the fact that they are allowing no balanced social interaction and that their self-centeredness does little to develop true friendship. Their role plays upon their unending goodness and kindness, so their victims are trapped by their own consciences, unless they themselves are exceptionally well-adjusted and can handle such situations with firmness and equanimity. Hopeless martyrs, the "Sick Pussycats" are most gratified when arousing extreme guilt or pity. They never outgrow the "so-and-so was mean to me" wail, like the small child who comes running home to Mommy complaining and moaning about the bad old teacher, when, in truth, the teacher did no more than ask him to turn in his homework.

It's probably apparent that few persons would have all the traits of one type or would be purely one type or the other. The dictator shrinks and cowers before a stronger dictator; the moderately rich braggart suddenly remembers to be modest when introduced to a prominent billionaire; the meek madonna bursts into a fury of fangs and claws if her child is threatened. And fiction has stereotyped the bellicose financier who is a roaring tiger in his office but who enjoys being pampered and babied at home. Most people draw somewhat from each type, and it must be remembered that human beings are unique individuals, not to be categorized like old campaign buttons or trading cards. However, most people fit into one type or the other more or less obviously, according to their prevailing method of overcoming their sense of inferiority.

It bears repeating that the less secure people are, the more noticeably their compensatory mechanisms come into play, mechanisms which, unfortunately, often produce rejection instead of validation, thereby triggering redoubled efforts by the compensatory mechanism. The victim of this inverse therapy digs himself deeper and deeper into his pit of low self-esteem.

A few unfortunate neurotics employ the most extreme compensatory techniques of both "Sick Tigers" and "Sick Pussycats," a strategy which strangles them in a disastrous double bind. These people want everything. They want to be both loved and feared. But obviously, no personality structure can survive the attempt to be a domineering tyrant and an ingratiating apple-polisher at the same time and place. Invariably the feedback of each behavior cancels out some desired result. Only the most skillful therapy can save them. But tragically, that part of their self-image which portrays the strong, superior, independent Tiger usually blocks any pleas for help.

Obviously, both extremes of these types have difficulty with interpersonal relationships, due not only to their basic insecurity but also to problems connected with each type. The Sick Tiger's practice of building himself up at the expense of others makes him unpopular. Feeling rejected and lonely, he automatically steps up his defenses, thereby generating even more unpopularity. On the other hand, the Sick Pussycat is sometimes well liked, but usually not enough to satisfy his insatiable appetite for approval. No matter how skilled his "people-pleasing" mechanism, he usually finds personal affiliations disillusioning because he expects more than most friends or relatives can give; his needs are never completely satisfied. Every new acquaintance must be a new conquest; every chance meeting must prove his social success. With so much energy expended to prove his popularity everywhere, he sometimes evolves into a "street angel, house devil." By the time he returns home, off stage as it were, he can no longer keep the act going, can no longer hide his all-too-human feelings. At home he lets all his feelings boil over, much to the pain of those nearest and dearest to him. Those who can play the part of angel every minute of their lives, both home and abroad, are in a still worse dilemma. Deprived of the luxury of ever expressing their antisocial emotions, these unfortunates must push their feelings into a hidden volcano, until eventually they erupt in some manner of intrapunitive or extrapunitive violence, deep depression, or other destructive neurosis.

The extremes of both types also function poorly in the parent role, because they retard the emotional growth of their children by discouraging independence. The Sick Tiger is determined to direct every move. His children live in a maze of "thou shalts" and "thou shalt nots," with never any freedom to make their own decisions and learn by means of their own failures or successes. The Sick Pussycat coddles his children, overprotecting and indulging them, so that they never experience the satisfaction of facing a challenge and thereby building self-respect. The offspring of both types are likely to feel inferior and insecure, though for different reasons.

No group has more cleverly applied Adler's theory to their own field than have the advertising media. In his *Hidden Persuaders*,[20] Vance Packard cites many examples of reaching the consumer through his desire to feel influential, important, and powerful. A certain tractor manufacturer found that despite a costly colored ad in a national magazine, sales were falling. The ad featured a photo taken at an angle which made the large, heavy tractor seem to bear down upon the small, helpless reader. This didn't work very well; in fact, business went backwards. So the picture was retaken from an angle over the shoulder of the driver, who then appeared large and strong in the foreground, in command of the monstrous machine. This ad, flattering the muscular masculinity of farmers, brought immediate results. In another instance, a life insurance company had thought to appeal to prospective buyers by portraying the easy comfortable pattern of life the family would achieve when the breadwinner was dead and gone to his "Happy Isle." However, psychological projective tests revealed that most men had a fierce desire to dominate their families even after their own deaths, that they purchased life insurance so that they would at least in one sense continue to control the standard of living and guide the education of their children. Therefore the life insurance company cleverly designed ads which showed Daddy as part of the family group, as the hero who, even though not physically present in the years to come, was still directing and governing by means of his wise provision.

As do the advertising media, you also can apply Adler's theory to a large portion of human behavior, thereby understanding your pained and bumbling fellow man with more clarity and tolerance. For example, a recent lovelorn column carried the following letter:

> What's wrong with my romance? Hal and I argue all the time. He gets mad if I beat him at tennis or Scrabble. He contradicts me in front of friends. He'd rather die than give me a compliment. Hal expects me to do small favors for him, but when I ask him to do something for me he says he's no errand boy. He wants to get married in April. What do you think?

Doubtless you are not the least bit puzzled about Hal; a person who must constantly prove himself superior in every way is suffering from an "inferiority complex." Unless Hal gets bashed in the head with some kind of insight, he will continue to make himself and everyone around him extremely miserable.

Nevertheless, if you should chance to meet Hal, and you probably will, you must resist the urge to perform this service for him. A certain university professor's opening address to a class in abnormal psychology always began something like this:

> This is a difficult course, but if you pass it with a good grade, you will know practically all anyone knows about abnormal psychology. You will know what is wrong with many of the people you meet. I now give you one never-to-be-broken command. DO NOT TELL THEM.

There are many ways a nonprofessional counselor may help others, but hanging diagnoses onto people is not one of them. Labels are dangerous for several reasons: they are dehumanizing, they may be inaccurate, and they may aggravate the condition. In addition, the lay counselor, after opening this Pandora's box, may not know what to do about it.

Because it receives much attention these days, and also because it's a very practical theory for the use of nonprofessionals, it would be appropriate to include a brief summary of Eric Berne's Transactional Analysis, extremely abbreviated and streamlined, with much of the theory deleted. The system has been so popularized that the terms involved have become household words. Basing the theory on those of Freud and the social psychologists who followed, Berne used simple, catchy language and diagrams. As Berne himself explained it,

> Each human being exhibits three types of ego states. (1) Those derived from parental figures, colloquially called the Parent. In this state, he feels, thinks, acts, talks, and responds just as one of his parents did when he was little. This ego state is active, for example, in raising his own children. Even when he is not actually exhibiting this ego state, it influences his behavior as the "Parental influence," performing the functions of a conscience. (2) The ego state in which he appraises his environment objectively, and calculates its possibilities and probabilities on the basis of past experience, is called the Adult ego state, or the Adult. The Adult functions like a com-

puter. (3) Each person carries within a little boy or little girl, who feels, thinks, acts, talks, and responds just the way he or she did when he or she was a child of a certain age. The ego state is called the Child. The Child is not regarded as "childish" or "immature," which are Parental words, but as childlike, meaning a child of a certain age, which may be anywhere between two and five years in ordinary circumstances. It is important for the individual to understand this Child, not only because it is going to be with him all his life, but also because it is the most valuable part of his personality.[21]

Perhaps this description of the three ego states: Parent, Adult, and Child, should be somewhat explained further. Actually it's logical to begin with the Child, for that ego state represents those qualities which we naturally bring into the world with us—spontaneity, intuition, creativity, and feelings endowed by nature. This ego state is the creative-emotional self. Soon after birth begins the parental guiding, nurturing, teaching, and admonishing. These shaping and molding messages, mostly verbal, are imprinted upon the growing child and become the Parent ego state. In this state we carry our attitudes toward work, religion, the law, and hundreds of other worldly situations and institutions. The third ego state, called Adult, really has little to do with age. It is the machinelike, factual reasoning process, aptly described as the computer. James and Jongward clarify the concept even more sharply.

The *Parent ego state* contains the attitudes and behavior incorporated from external sources, primarily parents. Outwardly, it often is expressed toward others in prejudicial, critical, and nurturing behavior. Inwardly, it is experienced as old Parental messages which continue to influence the inner Child.

The *Adult ego state* is not related to a persons's age. It is orientated to current reality and the objective gathering of information. It is organized, adaptable, intelligent, and functions by testing reality, estimating probabilities, and computing dispassionately.

The *Child ego state* contains all the impulses that come naturally to an infant. It also contains the recordings of his early experiences, how he responded to them, and the "positions" he took about himself and others. It is expressed as "old" (archaic) behavior from childhood.

When you are acting, thinking, feeling, as you observed your parents to be doing, you are in your Parent ego state. When you are dealing with current reality, gathering facts, and computing objectively, you are in your Adult ego state. When you are feeling and acting as you did when you were a child, you are in your Child ego state.[22]

One or two examples will illustrate how the ego states operate. The Adult might note, "The temperature this morning is 90 degrees." the Child might respond, "Gee! Going for a swim would be fun and would really feel good." The Parent might answer, "A warm day or not, it's my duty to get this work finished." The three ego states, all belonging of course to the same person, have noted the weather in their individual, characteristic ways. The Adult is simply computer-factual, the Child is spontaneous-emotional, the Parent is directive-ethical. Another example: The Adult might say, "I'm going to a movie tonight." The Child might think, "I hope it isn't scary." The Parent might think, "I hope it's not one of those naughty, immoral pictures."

Combined, these three states are called the personality structure, and separation of one from the other in any given behavior is called "Structural Analysis." "Transactional Analysis" means analyzing a communication, a transaction, between two persons. Berne felt that people get into difficulty when transactions get "crossed." In other words, when a response is expected from one ego state, and instead it comes from another. For instance, you might say to a friend, matter-of-factly, in your Adult, "I can't go to the show with you tonight; I have to work." You expect an Adult reply, something like, "I see. Can we plan to go another night?" But instead, he answers, "You don't seem to care whether I have to spend the evening alone or not." His petulant Child is answering, and you're probably both very uncomfortable.

One hears a lot about "parent tapes," phrases and attitudes which are spoken or acted out by actual parents which then become engrained in children to build their Parent ego state as a lifetime structure. There are many examples at hand at all times, such comments as "Candy will ruin your teeth," or "Girls should marry, stay at home and have babies," or "What will the neighbors think!" or "A college education is important if you expect to get anywhere," or "Boys don't cry." Some tapes are acted out. If parents go to church every Sunday, there's a tape which says something like, "Good people go to church." If parents spend a great deal of their leisure time reading, the tape says something like, "Reading is fun." Of course your particular tapes will be a different set, but think back carefully, and you'll find that you've been conditioned by hundreds of parental viewpoints and behavior. You'll probably also notice that you're a little edgy whenever you try to erase a certain tape by your speech or actions.

Parental tapes have much to do with the concept that a child forms about his own worth and about the worth of others around him. You've perhaps heard the expression "I'm OK, you're OK." What is the "OK" part all about? "OK" or "not-OK" refers to the psychological positions which people take toward themselves and toward others. When a child is very young, he begins to develop a concept about his own worth compared to other people's. To quote James and Jongward again,

When taking positions about themselves, people may conclude: I'm smart, I'm stupid, I'm powerful, I can't do anything right. . . . When taking positions about others, people may conclude. . . Nobody will give me anything, People are wonderful, People are no damn good, Someone will help me. . . .

In general the above positions are "I'm OK" or "I'm not-OK." The psychological positions taken about oneself and about others fit into four basic patterns. The first is the winner's position, but even winners may occasionally have feelings that resemble the other three.

The First Position: I'm OK, You're OK, is potentially a mentally healthy position. If realistic, a person with this position about himself and others can solve his problems constructively. . . .

The Second or Projective Position: I'm OK, You're not-OK, is the position of persons who feel victimized or persecuted. They blame others for their miseries. . . .

The Third or Introjective Position: I'm not-OK, You're OK, is a common position of persons who feel powerless when they compare themselves to others. This position leads them to withdraw. . . .

The Fourth or Futility Position: I'm not-OK, You're not-OK, is the position of those who lose interest in living. . . .

The person with the first position feels "Life is worth living." With the second he feels "Your life is not worth much." With the third he feels "My life is not worth much." With the fourth he feels "Life isn't worth anything at all."

As stated earlier, this brief glimpse of Transactional Analysis is oversimplified and omits much of the whole system. It serves only to give you a bare outline of the very highly organized theory.

Most personality theories emphasize that in the struggle to establish self-value, one's first experiences are important. Suffering rejection early in life is likely to give the child indelible feelings of inferiority;[23] on the other hand, experiencing pampering teaches him that he is too weak to fend for himself, molds him either into a manipulative, dependent personality, or into a hostile, self-centered personality, or into a blend of both. And most traumatizing of all is experiencing inconsistency—coddling one moment, punishment the next—so that the child lives in an unpredictable, chaotic nightmare.

From infancy onward a child is continuously gathering materials to build his impression of the world and also of his relationship to that world. At first the building stones are made up of emotional responses and feedback from the senses, but later on reasoning power comes into play. This structure will continue to grow throughout his lifetime, but more and more slowly as he becomes less curious and less involved. The foundation, the big heavy building stones of initial and most important truths in a child's life, is laid down earliest. Inasmuch as the human mind insists upon orderliness, a subsequent building stone which comes to hand will be rejected if it does not somehow "fit" or harmonize with the foundation. As these harmonizing stones are added here and there, one upon the other, it becomes more and more difficult to alter the underlying basic structure, style, or design.

"TAPES"

During your early years you have received and recorded certain messages. Psychologists have labeled these messages "tapes" or "scripts." You may have heard these messages verbatim, or you may have inferred the contents from behaviors or attitudes of authority figures. As a basic step in your process of knowing yourself and creating yourself as a secure, authentic person, go through this list of sample "tapes" and consider each one. If you have received the message, either directly or indirectly, mark it "+." If not, mark it "−."

1. It's more blessed to give than receive.
2. Don't take yourself and life too seriously.
3. Don't complain.
4. A thing worth doing is worth doing well.
5. Don't smoke.
6. You're not very good looking.
7. Don't be late.
8. The world is a pretty good place.
9. God won't love you if you're bad.
10. Daydreaming is a waste of time.
11. Do as you're told.
12. Think the best of people; accept them.
13. Don't indulge or pamper yourself.
14. Certain races or nationalities are inferior.
15. Good guys finish last.
16. Children should be seen and not heard.
17. Everything happens for the best.
18. You can't fight city hall.
19. Don't get angry.
20. Be yourself; act natural.
21. Save for your old age.
22. Music and art add wonderful dimensions to life.
23. People don't like you very much.
24. Don't drink alcoholic beverages.
25. Be courteous; good manners are important.
26. Girls should devote their lives to being good wives and mothers.
27. Admit your mistakes but don't brood over them.

28. Neatness is important.
29. Don't be vain.
30. Use your head.
31. Don't waste time.
32. Life is filled with problems; don't expect it to be always easy.
33. Everything in the Holy Bible is true.
34. If you are envious or jealous, you are not a good person.
35. You don't need a college education if your work doesn't require it.
36. Take good care of your body; practice good health habits.
37. This country is a rotten place to live.
38. You'll never amount to much.
39. Don't be a crybaby.
40. Don't criticize.
41. Certain religious groups want to take over.
42. Live by the Golden Rule.
43. The world of Nature is revitalizing and inspiring.
44. If you do a lot for people, they ought to be grateful.
45. You're rather stupid.
46. What will the neighbors think?
47. Don't trust anyone.
48. Don't gossip.
49. Life is exciting and challenging.
50. Going to church is important.
51. You have to accept the fact that no two people agree on everything.
52. A man should not express tender emotions.
53. Hardly anyone knows what he's talking about, even the experts.
54. Don't be proud.
55. Be honest with yourself.
56. Well-to-do people are usually snobs.
57. Don't be lazy. Worthwhile people work hard.
58. You should be grateful.
59. Will-power and self-discipline are important.
60. A college education develops you and makes life

more interesting.

61. Don't be supersensitive. You have to learn to be a good sport.
62. You're pretty.
63. A girl should remain a virgin until she's married.
64. When people treat you dirty, strike back.
65. Trust yourself and your own bent.
66. Money is power.
67. High principles are worth fighting for.
68. Manual labor is degrading.
69. Appearances are important.
70. Religious people are hypocrites.
71. Keeping clean is important.
72. You have to take care of yourself first.
73. Certain races want to conquer the world.
74. Everybody fails once in a while; don't let it get you down.
75. A husband should "rule the roost."
76. You have to learn to take criticism.
77. You're rather stupid.
78. Sex is dirty.
79. You should be able to solve your own problems.
80. Our political party is made up of intelligent, honest persons.
81. The other political party is made up of crooks and grafters.
82. 'Most everybody does the best he can.
83. Nice people don't hate anybody.
84. Be honest about expressing your feelings.
85. Keep your credit good.
86. Get involved in something you enjoy and you'll be happy.
87. It's important to live on the "right" side of the tracks.
88. You're a rare and wonderful person.
89. Employers get everything thay can out of you.
90. Have faith in yourself and others.
91. You're a mean person.
92. Don't blame other people when things go wrong.

93. Rich people got their money dishonestly. —
94. Don't worry about things you can't change. +
95. You don't know what you're talking about. +
96. People fail because they have bad luck. —
97. Accept yourself. +
98. Be kind and accepting of others. +
99. A man's masculinity is very important. —
100. You get whatever you really want out of life. +

Now look again at each item. Consider it carefully and decide whether you want to accept it totally, in part, or not at all. Make a stout affirmation accordingly. You will probably find it hard to erase the "tapes" marked "+."

Now again look at those tapes marked + and compare them. Do you find "double binds?" That is, do you find you have marked such tapes as "Act natural" and "Don't get angry" both with a +? Or both "Use your head" and "Do as you're told?" Many human insecurities have arisen from such double binds in parent tapes.

Lastly, make a list of your own parent tapes, almost anything you remember being said by authority figures when you were young. Decide how you feel about these comments or bits of advice.

In fact, once any building stone has been accepted and put into place, it isn't likely to be removed except by strong, deliberate decision. For one thing, its position is ratified over and over again, hundreds of times, by the mental and emotional process of association which prompts the self to relive the original lesson. To illustrate, a woman once complained that she was at a loss to understand why she panicked hopelessly whenever she tried to perform even the simplest piece of piano music if she knew someone was listening. Generally at ease even among strangers, this emotional reaction puzzled and embarrassed her. Upon being questioned she recalled her first experience at the keyboard. When she was five, she went along with her mother one afternoon to visit a friend. Noting her interest in the piano, the hostess kindly inquired, "Can you play the piano?" and the child, in the innocence of her years replied, "Oh yes." The hostess then invited her to perform. With quiet confidence the child accompanied herself, softly playing a few notes at random, as she sang in a true, clear voice her favorite Sunday school hymn, every verse from beginning to end,". . . He will gather the gems for His kingdom, all the pure ones, the bright ones . . . Little Children . . . His loved and His own." As she turned from the piano, expecting to be praised, she was instead frightened by the sight of her hostess in tears and her mother obviously upset. What she didn't know, and what no one explained to her, was that the woman's only son had recently been killed, and the whole scene, the child and the song itself, had tugged grievously at her emotions. Later at home, and often in the future, the mother recounted the whole incident, ridiculing the child's audacity in believing she knew how to play the piano. Each time the mother would laugh and scoff, "Of course, she didn't really know what she was doing." Probably the child relived her pain and embarrassment hundreds of times, not only when her mother repeated the story but when, through association, she was reminded of it perhaps by piano music, or the dress she had worn, or the dress her mother had worn, or certain words from the song, or Sunday school, or even the same weather or particular colors or moods or smells, or innumerable other reminders, however remote. The slightest clue would trigger the memories—her playing the piano, the hostess' tears, and her mother's scornful, "Of course, she didn't know what she was doing." The distressing lesson of her inferiority as a performing musician was hammered into her brain over and over again, finally to become a strongly cemented building stone in the child's psychic structure. It is no wonder that any attempt to perform at the piano aroused panic.

Beliefs acquired later in life have not been relived as often by means of association, have not in that way been "relearned" over and over again, nor have they been accepted in the same trusting way a child accepts his parents' teachings.

When a baby is born, his mother or surrogate mother is

his creator—omnipotent and omniscient. All-important in his life, it is she whose touch and voice and comings and goings first acquaint him with his environment, what it is like and how it receives him. A bit later his father will become more or less important, depending upon various circumstances. Still later, as the child gains mobility and more acute awareness, he will gather data from many sources, but for a long time his parents, especially his mother, will be the font of his impressions of the world. He will ignore or toss aside incongruent evidence, for he cannot entertain two conflicting ideas in the same place at the same time. He will hang onto that in which he has the most emotional investment, that is, parental attachment, and that which is reinforced by repetition or memory by association. For the sake of survival he will learn painful lessons the most quickly and thoroughly— that sharp knives hurt, that tall chairs used to reach cookie jars may tip over, that friends who are bitten may bite back. He will also quickly and thoroughly learn painful lessons about himself, especially if he is taught one way or another that he is unloved and unwanted. Lessons emphasizing his worthlessness and inferiority are the most traumatic and the most indelible of all.

Let us examine two contrasting examples in order to understand the effect of early experiences.

The subject of the first example is Mrs. Carroll, a woman born with a hideous facial disfigurement and double cleft palate which even extensive plastic surgery has done little to beautify. Her speech is marred by a repugnant impediment. Despite these handicaps which might have embittered her, Mrs. Carroll is well-adjusted emotionally and socially. Quite willing to discuss her life situation, she explains that she was lucky enough to have had both a mother and father who lavished affection and approval upon her, always encouraging her to meet the challenges of life with stout resourcefulness. From birth she was taught that her handicap was not all-important, that she was loved for herself, and, furthermore that her personality and multiple musical talents were special, rare blessings which were her responsibility to develop in order to enrich her life. With these solid foundation stones she built her impression of herself and her world, ignoring any incompatible stones occasionally thrown at her. Actually, the world gave her much positive reinforcement. Her zest for life attracted many friends, and if at a party there was a piano or a violin or a songfest, she was the star. She says that in her youth it occurred to her that in some ways her disfigurement was an asset; she was unique so that no one ever forgot her, and she never aroused jealousy. Discussing her difficulty in finding employment as a young girl, Mrs. Carroll expressed gratitude that her mother had taught her early in life that bruises and bumps were never to be taken as personal attacks. Like her mother before her, she is now a loving wife and mother, with few of the family crises which others complain about.

One can only guess how this woman's life might have turned out had her mother implanted a different attitude. Whereas some handicapped people are defensive, bitter, or dependent, this woman emanates the aura of her serene acceptance of the world as she finds it.

The second example is a direct contrast. Leon, age thirty-two, is now seeking professional help because of extreme chronic depression, so severe that he has twice attempted suicide. He feels that his fairly successful marriage is being threatened by his despondency and hot temper. Overly sensitive to criticism and quick to anger when others refuse to see things his way, he has quit several good jobs and been fired from one or two but has always been financially clever enough to "keep up a good front," which is important to him.

Leon's earliest recollection fastens upon a brief scene which took place when he was three years old. He was brought to "another foster home." Although he doesn't remember any previous home, he is positive he had no mother or father or other emotional ties at that time. His only feeling was an animal-like fear of the new situation. Neither the man in the black overcoat who brought him nor the heavy, limping old woman at the kitchen stove paid any attention to him. Leon can remember four more foster homes in the next one-and-a-half years, all much alike, wherein his predominant emotion was terror. He never called anyone Mother, was never cuddled or fondled as far as he can remember. Most often he was the charge of some unwilling teenager who expressed her resentment by baiting, tormenting, and harassing him. Upon one occasion, he was put to bed with a religious medal placed upon his chest. The next morning when it was found that the medal was not still in place, he was told, "God is very, very mad at you! He will punish you, you'll see. You're going to get a dreadful sickness and die!"

When he was four-and-a-half, his failing health began to alarm the visiting officials of the children's agency who were temporarily his legal guardians, so they placed him with a kindlier old couple out in the country. By this time he was gauntly underweight, subject to frequent attacks of vertigo and nausea, and already fighting the chronic depression which was to plague him right up to the present.

It is clear what kind of foundation building stones went into Leon's impression of his world and his relation to it. He could not avoid concluding that he was completely unwanted. He had no mother-god or father-god to defend his right to human existence; eventually even his own body betrayed him by its near collapse. Records at the children's agency showed that his mother had tried several times to abort her pregnancy before he was born. Shortly afterwards she had left him at the agency and then disappeared for about seven years. As the years went on, it could be expected that he would select building stones which fit his original concept. He would select each failure, each criticism, each negative reinforcement as further proof that he was a good-for-nothing.

What, you may ask, about Adler's theory of the primary drive in life, to overcome one's inferiority? The answer is that even Leon has not surrendered his instinct for survival, and so he must expend enormous energy to put the whole spectrum of defenses to work. Whereas self-confident people are like light, carefree gliders soaring easily on natural air currents of support, perfectly in balance with their surroundings, Leon, weighted by self-doubt, is like a heavy cumbersome airplane. He requires a steady, strong airstream of defenses to keep him afloat. If the motor is cut for even a moment, he begins to sink.

The most secure people realize that almost everyone has only average strengths and weaknesses. They also accept the fact that no one is completely free of anxiety. Ever since man ate of the tree of knowledge and thereby recognized the limitation and fragility of his existence, the flame of apprehension has burned within him, sometimes flaring hotly, sometimes smoldering imperceptibly, but never extinguished. Rollo May terms the smoldering type "normal anxiety" and goes on to explain,

> One can avoid "normal anxiety" only by buttoning himself up in a rigid dogma of superstition, religious belief, or an intellectual system. Primitive societies are less prone to anxiety (in our sense of the term) because of taboos which compel adherence to a pre-established mode of conduct, but the price of this is cultural stagnation and a thwarting of individual development. In a civilized society, good cannot be the complete absence of anxiety. It would be "crazy" not to have some anxiety.[24]

You may be unaware of the prevalence of anxiety, "normal" and otherwise, because one of the most universal behavioral defenses is the concealment of all forms of fear. Deep within the mechanism of the survival instinct which says that weakness is the first evil and strength the first good is the belief that any timidity, such as lack of self-assurance, must be hidden at all costs, even from those most trusted, sometimes even from the self. In our culture men especially feel obliged to hide their apprehension, for strength and courage are considered their special properties, their most identifying virtues. This determination to appear strong explains why fewer men than women accept help for emotional and interpersonal problems, although their needs are urgent, as witnessed by their high suicide rate. Many men, reluctant to admit they are entangled in problems they are incompetent to handle alone, wear perpetual camouflages of self-confidence.

Those in closest contact with other people's intimate

emotions—psychologists, ministers, psychiatrists, counselors, and social workers—often observe that the degree of anxiety suffered by a person tends to correlate with his degree of inferiority feelings. Lack of self-esteem heightens every kind of anxiety ranging from undefined free-floating anxiety to all types of painful insecurity, including physical fears. Those people who truly think well of themselves are relaxed, optimistic, trusting and venturesome. Their anxiety is at the minimum. They can live lightly and freely.

No matter how we look at human beings, their greatest need, their greatest good, is self-esteem.

8.

Mate Counseling

About ninety-eight percent of counseling could be termed "mate counseling." Although much of this involves married couples, the term "marriage counseling" seems inappropriate because there are also many cases of counseling for couples going "steady," widows who've lost their spouses, divorcees, L.T.A.'s (living together arrangements), single persons (as young as eighth graders) who feel rejected by a particular member of the opposite sex, or who're looking desperately for a member of the opposite sex to love. All these fall into the category of "mate counseling." To paraphrase Plato, it seems as though male and female are two pieces of a jigsaw puzzle, never feeling complete and content until rejoined, always "longing to grow into one."[25]

Sometimes the initial stages of counseling do not reveal sexual implications. During wartime some years ago Ella, a nineteen-year-old girl, consulted her family physician about a painful inflammation of her eyes and throat. The doctor performed all sorts of tests but despite the obvious redness could find no evidence of disease. Convinced that the symptoms were functional rather than organic, he told me about the case and asked if I could talk to the girl. I was immediately struck by her obvious dejection. Ella lived in cramped, shabby quarters with her foreign-born widowed mother who spoke little English. Although quite attractive, the girl had almost no social life for she was shy and too apologetic about her living conditions to bring acquaintances home. Due to her ailment she'd lost her factory job which had been dull and depressing anyway. After establishing rapport and learning of her life situation, I arranged to see her the following week. Then I checked with a nearby U.S.O. club where lessons in ballroom dancing were being offered to servicemen. The director assured me that if Ella knew her left foot from her right and was fairly good-looking, she would be hired as an instructor. The prospect of being in a position where she would automatically meet many attractive men made her spirits skyrocket. She reported for work without delay, the first day wearing dark glasses to screen her reddened eyes. Almost overnight there was no need for such camouflage. All signs of eye and throat irritation disappeared. Even though no specific mate was involved in this counseling situation, it was certainly a case of "mate counseling," for Ella's pain was traceable to her loneliness and longing for attention from the opposite sex.

In another case a twenty-year-old, Doreen, was brought to me by her troubled parents. Doreen had been under the care of several different therapists, one after the other, but none could prevent her continued suicide attempts, about six so far. She was withdrawn and appeared somewhat schizoid, although no diagnosis had been confirmed. Despite her protests that nothing had gone amiss in her boy-girl relationships, I intuited her need for close association with a male and called upon a male counselor to work with her while I continued to work with the other members of the family, all of whom were being affected by Doreen's aberrant behavior.

Some weeks later a young man with whom Doreen had previously been involved returned to the area, and the two resumed their intimate friendship. Whereupon Doreen shed all symptoms of emotional illness. She appeared to be absolutely cured and completely happy. Unfortunately, the parents promptly cancelled all professional help. It would have been wiser to let their daughter continue counseling sessions so that from her more healthy viewpoint she could have learned to understand herself and to strengthen her ego against future stress or threat.

Although neither Ella nor Doreen seemed to recognize her prime need in life, many other sad and lonely people are fully aware of their desire to love and be loved. Computer dating services wring fortunes out of this collective heartache. Books with titles such as *How to Pick Up Men* or *You, Too, Can Be Popular* go through several printings at great speed. And counselors often hear the comment, "I just can't stand this loneliness," or "What I need most is love and affection." Those persons who are widowed, whether by death or divorce, are seldom completely consoled until the vacancy is filled by another mate. Unfortunately, in their desperation they often quickly gamble their happiness on the first marriage or L.T.A. offer in the running, without pausing long enough to consider the betting odds.

Those who do have a mate find that their most painful source of unhappiness comes from discord in the relationship. Many persons find themselves in the dilemma of "I can't live with him/her, but I can't live without him/her." They often seem to be vacillating between divorce and murder.

Sometimes a troubled couple realizes that if they don't seek help from a trained, objective outsider, their marriage will go from bad to smashup. They usually begin the counseling session with a barrage of blaming—"He's so dictatorial, he thinks he knows it all." "She's still a mama's girl." "He thinks he can treat me like dirt in the rest of the house and then put me in a loving mood in the bedroom." "She's lazy and disorganized." And so it goes. Seldom, if ever, does either spouse say, "Even though we once loved each other very much, now our marriage isn't going well. What can I do about it?" Instead each mate, by this time feeling battered and bruised by real or imagined abuses of the other, is eager to prove the debacle is not his fault. Neither realizes that marriages are not repaired by sifting out who's right and who's wrong, a futile, destructive pastime. Counselors never seek to place blame or to administer verbal spankings, only to promote insight, understanding, and active communication.

As in every relationship, "character is destiny," and the destiny of a marriage depends upon the characters of the persons involved. Most importantly, each partner must have the integrity to honor the commitment implicit in every marriage—*the commitment to help fulfill each other's basic needs for love, health, a sense of self-worth, and a trusting relationship*. Invariably the marital relationship suffers when one or both mates grow indifferent to the other's basic needs.

Prior to marriage this matter of needs usually doesn't become evident because the courtship ritual itself fulfills mutual needs of the moment. The dating game is exciting, novel, suspenseful, romantic, teasing, adventuresome, and ego-building. Unfortunately our present culture provides very little postmarital ritual designed to build and bind the relationship. As a rule, partners get wedded for very human but very selfish reasons. Each looks to the other for, in addition to basic needs, lavish attention, emotional security, physical pleasure, financial gain, and entertainment. Frustrated and disappointed when the partner fails to magically provide these treasures, each begins the subtle or not so subtle attack. Often the battle continues until the wounds cannot be bound up and the relationship dies.

When couples come to me for help, I usually make a sketch of a four-poster, saying, "Let's check out the mate bed, one feature at a time. Right now the mattress, the symbol of all the love interchange, both physical and spiritual, is pretty wobbly, slanting this way and that." The diagram helps to serve their memories for future discussion when the couple returns home. Besides, the bed serves as a concrete symbol as they try to think positively about a firm love relationship.

The four legs of the bed have to do with verbal

interactions—Communication-sending, Communication-receiving, Negotiation, and Validation.

In earlier chapters we have reviewed the skills of Communication-sending: expressing one's feelings in a low-key way, without blaming or getting into head-trip arguments. The couple should be certain they know how to exercise this particular skill. If not, they must learn.

Communication-receiving is reflective listening, thinking along with the speaker, which has also been explained earlier. The listener is attentive and gives the kind of feedback which indicates his concern and understanding. Again, each spouse must learn to master this segment of communication, the second leg of the bed.

The third leg is Negotiation, an impressive sounding word which you might think applies to only very important issues. But actually a successful marriage depends very much upon constantly negotiating ordinary day-to-day decisions, very small ones as well as very large ones. Negotiation should be used for deciding whether a window is to be open or closed, which TV program is to be selected, or which dinner invitation is to be accepted, as well as which house or car is to be purchased. Of course small decisions don't have to be formal, complicated processes. A simple question such as, "Is it O.K. with you if I close the window?" and the answer "Fine," is a complete and satisfactory Negotiation. And it makes both mates feel much more congenial and loving than if one of them had slammed the window shut without consulting the other. Most important, every decision should be a fair, no-lose choice, each person deriving as much benefit as possible without jeopardizing the happiness of the other. Perhaps the window Negotiation could have been better settled by one person's putting on a sweater.

In a truly loving relationship each partner is more concerned for the welfare of the other than for himself, neither one strongly pushing for his own way except when he feels an extreme need. In such a case, instead of expecting his spouse to be a mind reader, he would honestly and openly explain this need, always keeping in mind that the relationship is more important than either mate's determination to have his own way. In most love relationships there is ample room for give-and-take which harms neither person; mature mates realize that very few controversial issues or material desires are all-important. Almost every decision can be negotiated without permanent damage to either person's well-being. For instance, a man might feel very strongly against his wife's wearing a bikini in public. His attitude might be difficult to explain rationally, but he would admit his emotional hang-up to his wife, asking for her cooperation. In such an instance the wife would realize that her entire happiness does not really depend upon her wearing a bikini, so rather than upset her husband or cause him discomfort, she would forego the pleasure it might give her to show off her faultless figure. However, if the marriage has degenerated to an ego-building power struggle instead of a partnership, the wife would defiantly wear the stringy little suit to prove her supremacy over her husband. In which case the husband would probably lose no time in finding some way to retaliate, so that the whole relationship would become a seesaw of revenge rather than a seesaw of giving and loving.

Sometimes couples agree to the principle of Negotiation, then proceed to turn it into a farce. A man agrees to pick up his own clothes if his wife will agree to mow the lawn. Or a wife agrees to stop acting seductive at parties if her husband will agree to take her out to dinner twice a week. Such Negotiations are not "fair, no lose choices," they're blackmail. A fair-minded husband would expect to pick up his own clothes in any case, and a fair-minded wife would not expect to seduce other men at parties or anywhere else. A deep, enduring love cannot be built upon childish games. Almost unbelievably, marriages have been known to break up ostensibly over quarrels about who would feed the cat (time expended per day for this task, three minutes) or which side of the garage belonged to whom as a parking space (no difference between the two spaces). Of course such issues are never really the basic reason for divorce.

Many couples protest that they have nothing in common, nothing to build their relationship upon. In truth, they have every act of their daily lives in common, hundreds of experiences, responses, ideas, and ideals which interweave. And every Negotiation, large or small, is a thread of shared feelings and attitudes which draws them closer together. Naturally, each mate may not want to participate in every decision. The husband may want the wife to decide what daily menu to serve, or the wife may want the husband to decide how a sprinkler system should be installed. But even this hands-off agreement is one type of shared Negotiation.

Some Negotiations require long discussion with much active listening and careful compromise, perhaps those concerning the handling of money. In some partnerships one member of the duo can't resist immediate gratification of every tempting desire—clothes, cars, trips, sports equipment—and has an irresponsible, reckless attitude toward impending bankruptcy. The other mate may simply want to establish a firm credit rating, or may be a penny-pinching neurotic, or, worse, may also want to indulge a desire to own everything in sight. In any event, if the art of Negotiation has not been mastered, money can cause many nasty disputes. But so can child rearing, in-law troubles, fighting crabgrass, or anything else.

Sometimes a discouraged husband or wife will remark to me, "I just think I'll give up the whole relationship and find someone else more reasonable." Of course a counselor never gives advice, but I'm always tempted to point out that flexible give-and-take must occur in any marriage, no matter how often one changes partners. Fair, loving Negotiation is important to keep the mate-bed steady—to provide a feeling of harmony and close communion.

The final "leg" is Validation. Validation means making a person feel good about himself; it means promoting self-esteem. Everyone in the world needs a great deal of it. The most traditional Validation is to say, "I love you." Praise is also an important kind of Validation, not only praise for accomplishment, but praise for just being. It's nice to hear someone say, "You did a great job on the pigpen," or "Nobody can make bumbleberry biscuits like yours;" but it's even better to hear that person say, "Gee, it's good to see you home early; I really miss you," or "Marrying you has made me feel that I'm the luckiest guy in the world," or "We always have so much fun together," or "You're really a jewel!" or "I knew when I first saw you that you were someone I'd like to know better," or "I'd rather be with you than with anyone in the world." There are dozens of ways of expressing the idea that someone is a rare and marvelous being. Everyone is unique and wonderful; he doesn't have to earn a Bronze Star or an Academy Award to deserve recognition of his value.

In addition, there are other even more discreet and effective methods of Validation. For example, a person always feels worthwhile when his opinions or advice are sought. Everyone enjoys hearing a sentence which begins, "What do you think about ————————?" whether it concerns an important political issue, or which color paint to use, or how a comic strip serial will turn out. Such a statement says, "I value you, so I value your opinions and viewpoints; furthermore, understanding them will make me understand you and feel closer to you." A person who loves another deeply will want to learn of his interests, attitudes, tastes, anxieties, philosophies, and many other areas of his personality. Another kind of Validation says, "You are so important to me that I'm thinking of you constantly." This thought is conveyed by small gifts, not necessarily involving expense, or by statements such as, "I saw the most beautiful sweater in the store window today, just your shade of blue," or "I was so sorry you weren't with us at the beach today; you'd have loved it." Another kind of Validation says, "You deserve to be happy, so I'll make certain our time together is enjoyable. I'll save up bits of interesting news or amusing events or anecdotes. I'll be lively, amiable and imaginative, focusing on you instead of me." We all experience Validation, that is, feel good about ourselves, when someone makes an effort to be good company. It's the secret of successful hospitality. Although it sounds easy, it takes intelligence, imagination, and a willing heart.

As I discuss the four "legs" with couples, they often understand the principles but find them difficult to put into practice. Therefore, I usually suggest that they engage in role-playing, acting out situations which demonstrate how they handle their feelings. Even more revealing is "role reversal," each one playing the other's role. Both these exercises help the partners to become discerning about their own behavior and its effect on each other.

If both mates understand and can practice the four skills represented by the four legs, I move on to explain the frame of the bed, which represents Maturity. Like any frame, it has four sides, all interdependent. These four sides of Maturity are Self-Esteem, Acceptance of Others, Sense of Humor, and Sense of Honesty. They add up to Maturity, without which any interpersonal relationship is extremely shaky. Practically every divorce can be traced to lack of some aspect of Maturity.

For example, without Self-Esteem, without loving himself, a person is simply incapable of loving another with complete abandon; too much of his effort is bent toward defending his own ego, searching for his own security. Most likely he's touchy and supersensitive, imagining all kinds of insults and put-downs or attaching undue importance to the least rejection or slight. He tends to be demanding, blaming, critical, bullying, suspicious, or self-pitying. Almost anything but loving. Only after gaining a measure of sense of self-worth with its guarantee of strength and confidence can a person love another, freely and generously.

For anyone who needs to build up his Self-Esteem, I put several lessons from this book to work. To begin with, the mastery of communication skills is the most direct path to feelings of self-confidence and self-worth. A person who interacts honestly and empathetically with other people soon grows to accept himself in the same way he accepts others. Further, if he acquires the habit of validating other people, as explained on the previous pages, he will be pleasantly surprised to find how much he feels the same validation radiated back to him. When a person acts or speaks in a way that emphasizes the best in another human being, he is like sunlight flashing onto a mirror; the glow is reflected.

In addition, a person seeking to build up his self-acceptance should take account of his "parent tapes," deciding for himself which values he chooses, which he rejects. He can begin with those listed in this book, and follow the directions he finds there. Much lack of Self-Esteem stems from the many double binds in our personal collection of parent tapes, double binds which have never been sorted out logically. One tape says, "Be yourself, act natural;" another says, "Don't be a crybaby." How can anyone obey both? One tape says, "Live by the golden rule;" another says, "Good guys finish last." How can anyone believe both and survive emotionally? Many parent tapes discourage feelings of self-worth simply because they contain built-in feelings of guilt and inferiority. A particularly cruel one is, "Don't be vain." People who are hooked on this one feel guilty if they have their teeth straightened or buy a new pair of shoes. I've had clients who desperately needed plastic surgery, but their "Don't be vain" training wouldn't allow it. Another one is, "Don't be proud." This means you're supposed to pretend you do everything for the good of mankind, nothing just for the fun or glory of it. I know one daring hunter who has braved some of the most dangerous slopes in Alaska, but he can't admit to himself or to anyone else that his courage and sportsmanship make him proud of himself. He has to attribute the trips to some lofty motives, all of which is very confusing to his friends. Anyone who examines these two exhortations carefully might have the spunk to ask, "What's wrong with a little self-respect and pride? Actually, both traits are quite civilizing." Many of our punitive standards of behavior make us responsible for other people or force us to deny our most natural feelings. As adults we should face the truth that we can't, for instance, always be our brother's keeper nor can we always suppress feelings of anger when we are hurt or threatened.

Once a person examines all his personal rules and regulations and attitudes and selects those that are right and reasonable for him, he can learn to live with a minimum of guilt by the logical code he's adopted. He can admit he's human, admit he has human defenses, fears, and frailties. What a relief that will be!—both to himself and to those who love him. For with new inner freedom he will begin to savor his personal authenticity and build a solid Self-Esteem.

A second side of the four-poster frame is Acceptance of Others, open mindedness. This means accepting the other person, just as he is, allowing him to have his quirks and biases. Many couples feel personally threatened if they do not concur in every belief and viewpoint, forgetting that a person who does not think for himself has no more substance than a shadow. A spouse may not agree in the matter of religion, philosophy of education, politics, or artistic taste. Which guarantees stimulating discussion during long winter evenings.

The third side of the frame is Sense of Humor, the ability to "live lightly," to have a sense of proportion and perspective, to enjoy the small gifts of each moment. Sense of humor does not mean a ha-ha gift of wit; in fact many witty persons have no Sense of Humor at all. They take themselves so seriously that they must always be center stage, and any failure to command applause and attention is a calamity. A person with a Sense of Humor can take the bitter with the better, realizing we all get more or less of both. He can watch with equanimity his own occasional failure or embarrassment, accepting his own humanness along with everyone else's. He keeps his spirit up most of the time, because he knows the choice of moods is his and a genial heart makes life more joyful.

The fourth side of the frame is Honesty. This means Honesty with oneself and others. It's difficult to understand and relate to another person while trying to disguise one's own motivations or intentions. However, Honesty is sometimes painful. In our guilt-ridden culture it's difficult to admit to selfishness, hate, vanity, and all those other human traits we ordinarily try to sweep under the rug. But in the long run it's a relief to say, "Yes, I've got them to a degree, so I accept the fact. Accepting them in myself, I can tolerate them in other people without feeling outraged."

Couples who check out the mate-bed and sincerely try to repair it and make it sturdy learn to share their lives with appreciation and generosity of spirit. They learn that "love" is an active verb, and that marriage or any love relationship is a priceless structure which they themselves create and then cherish.

But this realization is not easily brought about. The marriage counselor must have not only a thorough academic training, but the natural tact, intuition, and finesse of a U.N. peace delegate. Each mate is defensive, sensitive to the slightest hint that you may be siding with the other person. When he/she thinks, or imagines this is happening, the conjoint counseling sessions are doomed. Over and over the counselor must impress upon the couple that counseling is a nonjudgmental matter of education.

Often one spouse, most usually the husband, refuses to see a counselor. He's been brought up to believe that strong, intelligent people always solve their own problems, and going to a counselor is an admission of weakness and failure. Further, there is the fear that somehow he will be blamed and will be coerced to make some painful personality changes which will somehow deprive him of his masculinity. Sometimes the wife can persuade him to accompany her to a counselor by pointing out that although he can solve all his problems, she's unable to solve hers. Therefore, she needs his support and help; one way he can help is to accompany her to the counselor's office. His participation, if any, will be entirely voluntary. His viewpoints will be welcomed, but if he prefers he may assume the role of bystander. He is even free to excuse himself in the middle of a session; no one will question him. Many husbands will cooperate this much in order to protect the marriage and usually under these circumstances, they gain insights which improve the relationship.

Sometimes the wife must abandon the idea of persuading the husband to accompany her and must then get counseling by herself. Often this turns out to be more effective than she'd dreamed, for the wisdom she gains benefits her in many ways. For one thing, she learns that the discord is not all her fault, that her husband, like everyone, has a pattern of personality defenses which makes him behave in certain ways—ways which have nothing to do with her. This knowledge removes much of the tension between the two. Further, the wife learns how to bring out the best in her husband, how to build him up, how to protect his ego. Learning to understand him makes her love him more, makes her more patient and empathetic. Many, many times a wife has said to me, "You know, it's strange. I'm the one coming to you, but my husband seems to be the one who's changing." She's unaware that a personal interaction is like the balance of a weigh scale—a different weight, or pull, on one side invariably affects the other side. A good marriage is a matter of complement and balance.

Generally speaking, mate counseling falls into three main categories of problem situations.

In the first category, and in these times the most prevalent, the wife is discontented with the role she has been assigned in the marriage. She seeks an equal partnership, which she interprets as meaning that both mates will share the household duties, opportunities to work outside the home, and companionship. Sometimes none of this has been discussed before marriage, the woman assuming that her beloved concurs in her beliefs. Or sometimes it has been discussed superficially, the man agreeing vaguely to all his fiance's cute talk about equality and modern woman's freedom. He's never really analyzed the implications in detail. After marriage the wife either continues her full-time job or she becomes a mother. In any case she is expected to pick up after the husband, do the cooking, laundering, and cleaning, and then be content to work on her stitchery while her husband reads the sports section and watches TV. If she pleads, "Talk to me," he answers confusedly, "What about?" The wife can't understand why she's been demoted (from her point of view) to servant status; the husband can't understand what he's supposed to say in order to develop the "deep, meaningful relationship" the wife hungers for. Most often, the man sees himself as a strong, steady, protector and provider, a heroic role. Often he's not very verbal, especially about feelings and motivations, a kind of conversation which to him belongs in a woman's world. His own talk centers mostly on machinery or sports, subjects understood mainly by men. In all this he's usually very much like his father, who has served as teacher and model for about two decades, so that the behavior grooves have been carved deep into the son's psyche. The wife sees herself as intelligent and interesting, worthy of the close companionship and continual attentions of her mate. Modern cultural trends have taught her that she deserves a flexible choice of significant roles in life and that housework is demeaning.

Of course there are many variations on the outline of this drama, but the basic plot presents itself over and over. Usually, it's resolved in one of several ways. The wife may endure the situation without much protest until apathy sets in. Apathy, the most dangerous threat to a relationship, is like a pearl fashioned around an irritating grain of sand. It grows silently, internally, one of Nature's beautiful protections. Like the oyster, the relationship must be destroyed to get rid of it. In other cases the wife, feeling she can no longer tolerate the situation, demands sudden, radical changes in husband's behavior. He, essentially very much in love with his wife, attempts an overnight metamorphosis which is a sudden, traumatic onslaught to his ego and causes emotional upheaval, perhaps damage. In still other instances the wife goes alone for professional help and gains enough understanding, about both her husband and herself, to improve the conjugal relationship. In the most ideal situation, both partners seek help and work together in a way which produces the most growth and contentment for both.

Some years ago Miriam, a housewife and mother, came to me complaining that her husband was domineering, demanding, and unfeeling. As she saw it, he failed to provide any companionship, often finding excuses to be with his men friends instead of staying home or taking her out for an evening. He was also critical, not only of her but of their two teenagers. She felt her life was a dull routine of housework, with little reward or excitement. She'd tried some part-time jobs but, not having any marketable skills, could not find work which was satisfying. Immediately we began to focus on the skills of verbal interaction, keeping in mind her children as well as her husband. Miriam was an amazingly apt pupil. Soon she discovered that not only could she practice the intriguing principles of good communication herself, but she could also subtly indoctrinate the whole family with the same ideas. While she was doing all this at home, she was also learning during our counseling sessions to understand and appreciate her husband so that much of his behavior, which at one time had seemed intolerable, now seemed human and acceptable. Miriam also learned that much of what she'd thought was her husband's problem was really her own. As a result of all her newfound wisdom, her marriage smoothed out perceptibly. And then a happy turn of events tumbled a new project in Miriam's lap. She became associated with a little theater group and discovered that she had quite a nice talent for acting. Whereupon, so preoccupied was she with the flurry of tryouts, rehearsals, costumes, opening nights, and cast parties that there was no space in her life for discontent. Best of all, her husband also found room for his talents in the venture, designing and building sets, so that he shared his wife's enthusiastic involvement. He was also proud of her stardom, applauding louder than anyone whenever she was onstage!

The second oft-recurring category of mate counseling concerns the couples who simply lack enough emotional security to honor the commitments demanded of a satisfactory marriage. Each person has such an irresistible drive to satisfy his own needs for ascendancy, whether by manipulation or domination, that he cannot cater to his partner's basic needs. Usually, but not always, these couples are very young, still uncertain about their own identity and self-esteem. They are supersensitive, often feeling rejected or threatened. Their situation is sometimes made even more difficult by money problems, interfering relatives, or a nonalignment of values.

Some couples, recognizing their own emotional immaturity, seek to avoid the complications of marriage and a possible divorce by refusing to participate in any legal contract, agreeing to an L.T.A. (living together arrangement) instead. Usually such couples call attention to the freedom they'll enjoy. They brag, "It'll be great! We'll share everything only as long as we feel like it." This sounds ideal. No commitments, no promises, no responsibilities; no plan anyone will have to carry out if he's not in the mood. Simple! But whatever else it may be, life is never simple. What do they do about the apartment lease? Who is stuck with it? Who owns the furniture? Does a woman carry a pregnancy to full term? Or might the guy be up and away at the last minute? Sometimes they agree that one of the partners should go back to school. He quits a good job, registers for classes, and then the other partner leaves the scene. Saddest of all is the emotional trap. At first the whole arrangement is light and carefree, but gradually one partner realizes he can't bear to lose the other. All day at work he worries that when he gets home, he'll find a half-empty clothes closet, and a goodbye note where the stereo used to be. The strain grows worse and worse until it becomes insufferable. His head tells him he isn't married, but his heart isn't paying any attention. Finally there's a big blow up of hurt and anger, which destroys any possibility of a peaceful resolution. Aware of what's happening around them, some L.T.A.ers have settled on a verbal contract. They agree that no matter what happens, they'll stick with it for a certain length of time—a month, two months, or even a year. This allows them the security to make plans and not to worry that their whole life situation is going to disintegrate overnight. One can predict that the contracts might get longer and longer; they might even be called "marriage."

The third category of mate counseling concerns persons who are looking for a mate. Some have lost a mate; some have never been married. Often these are people who feel they have a wide circle of friends, but no valuable, close relationships.

Very often they beg to know, "Where can I find a woman? (or a man). How can I attract the person I want? Really now, what is the secret ingredient of popularity?" In their desperate loneliness many of these people go about solving their problem in all the wrong ways. Perhaps every potential mate they meet they try to overwhelm with attention, favors, or gifts. Or they try to impress everyone with their perfection, or their intelligence. Or they try to be continuously entertaining, with a steady stream of talk, brilliant or otherwise. Or they immediately get tense and personal, trying to push the relationship faster than normal. Or they play the whimpering "poor me" role. Of course, any of these tactics serve only as a hard wind to drive any potential friendship out of sight to a distant shore. Few of us have a receptive attitude toward people who make us feel indebted, inferior, overshadowed, threatened, or pitying. These are uncomfortable feelings. Instead, we're attacted to people who make us feel relaxed and comfortable, people who are natural, warm, spontaneous, accepting, and human.

If you look around you at the persons who always seem to have a steady supply of admirers, you'll notice that most of them seem to observe certain rules which make them charming and companionable. For one thing, they seem to have mastered the communication skills. Because they are sincerely interested, they do a lot of active listening; at the same time they are not shy about expressing their own honest feelings and attitudes in a nonblaming, matter-of-fact way. They say what they have to say unselfconsciously, briefly, and to the point, leaving out unnecessary details and repetition.

Furthermore, you'll notice that really personable people seldom keep the spotlight focused on themselves very long. Their self-esteem is so high that they don't need to spend a lot of time proving themselves. In fact, in their enthusiasm for life, they seem to forget all about themselves, so there's no pretense, no supersensitivity, no demands for attention. They're relaxed and natural.

Accepting themselves, these people can wholeheartedly accept others. Inasmuch as they don't expect perfection, their talk is seldom centered upon criticism, complaint, or ridicule. They realize that all of us are pretty much like children, stumbling and bumbling along through life, all doing the very best we can for wherever we're "at." They exercise a broad, easygoing understanding of the human condition. Perhaps their most salient quality is their ability to make other people feel good about themselves. They have a knack for validation, for bringing out the best in everyone, for conveying their consideration and respect for each person they meet.

In addition, you'll learn that likable people are interesting, most often because they've found some consuming, exciting interests in life. They are deeply fascinated and involved in something outside themselves and their families. The project may have intellectual, creative, or artistic basis; it doesn't matter which. Each self-actualized person seeks his own fascination, his own "thing," so that each new day is greeted with sharp anticipation.

You'll also notice that well-liked people usually live lightly, spontaneously, joyously, not taking themselves too seriously. To put it simply, they're good company. They tend to laugh easily and often enjoy the wit and imagination of their Child ego state. They don't worry much; they have neither the inclination nor the time.

You'll probably make a final observation about those who are loved; seldom do they set out deliberately and selfishly to find a mate. Love is most often a by-product of a genuine interest and acceptance of the world and the people in it.

TWENTY QUESTIONS

When we really care about someone, we find out about that person. We inquire, listen, discuss, observe, and intuit. Of the hundreds of bits of information which any caring person would want to know about his beloved, here are a few.

1. What would she/he appreciate most for a gift?
2. What cheers her/him up and makes her/him feel loved and worthwhile?
3. What are his/her likes and dislikes in music, art, entertainment?
4. In his/her work, what are the rewards and what are the tribulations?
5. What does it take to hurt his/her feelings deeply?
6. What does he/she feel about religion, church, concept of God?
7. Is she/he a romantic or a realist?

8.Does he/she have any long-standing anxieties? What are they?

9.What is her/his favorite reading matter? Favorite writers? Favorite flower? Favorite food? Favorite sport? Favorite color?

10.Is her/his self-esteem high or low? In what areas does she/he feel insecure?

11.What prejudices does she/he have? What are her/his views on busing and racial integration? Mixed marriages?

12.If he/she could take a vacation trip to anywhere in the world, where would it be?

13.What kind of surroundings bring out the best in her/him?

14.By nature is she/he an extrovert or an introvert?

15.What does she/he consider desirable qualities in a member of the opposite sex? Appearance? Sense of humor? Honesty? Trust? Gentleness? "Class?" Business ability?

16.What guilt feelings is she/he harboring?

17.What makes him/her really depressed or discouraged?

18.If he/she had three magic wishes, what would they be?

19.What was the most important event of her/his life between the ages of one and seven? What "peak" experiences has she/he had so far in life?

20.How does she/he feel about children and child-rearing? Is he/she authoritarian? Permissive?

9.

Crisis Counseling

No matter what your role in the helping professions, whether you are a telephone worker for a "suicide and crisis" service, a paraprofessional in a rehabilitation center, an empathetic person who avails himself to his friends in trouble, or whatever, you probably secretly fear your own inadequacy in the face of an ominous emergency, such as a suicide threat or a suicide attempt. No doubt your first move if the situation permitted, should be to seek the help of a professional. The many reasons for this advice are obvious, so there is no necessity to point them out. However, you may find yourself in a situation where such help is not available, so whatever information you can glean here will be useful.

Statistics indicate that about 90 percent of serious suicide attempts are abortive. The would-be suicides are rescued by speedy emergency procedures; or else they bumble their death tries, whether by accident or design no one is certain. Ten percent of the suicide attempts do result in death, but there is much convincing evidence that many people who kill themselves do not honestly intend to do so; they are victims of their own miscalculation. A relative whom they expect to return home in time to save them fails to appear. A telephone on which they depend does not function properly at the last moment. In truth one of the characteristics of the suicidal person is a certain ambivalence, an inability to choose between life and death.

Although the wish to live is a strong instinctual drive, the wish to die is, at least temporarily, almost as strong, due to a variety of motivations. Perhaps there is a desire to escape pain or insurmountable problems, or a desire to punish— both the self and the persons around the self—or there are drives which the person himself does not understand. You, the counselor, can help defeat the suicide effort by stimulating the universal drive for self-preservation, no matter how weak it may be at the moment.

You must recognize several stages in the handling of any suicide threat, no matter whether it has minimal or highly lethal potentiality. The first stage is the initial contact with the would-be suicide. Your attitude toward the threat is an important part of your effectiveness. You must school yourself to build rapport from the beginning, not allowing yourself to evidence shock, extreme anxiety, or a moralistic attitude. Frequently the suicide looks to you to help solve his problems or alter his mood; therefore, any emotional inadequacy on your part contributes to his sense of hopelessness or despondency. Although you should not express excessive anxiety, it is important that you do express genuine concern. The suicide very often feels that the world in general is indifferent, that he has no importance or significance. At the moment you may be the only person in the universe he feels he can trust and relate to. It is also important that you get any vital information as quickly as possible, especially if this is a telephone contact where you cannot observe the person's behavior directly. Suicide prevention often depends upon prompt action, but sometimes a suicidal person delays his explicit call for help, while he plays a deathly game of cat-and-mouse with his own life.

If a suicide is currently being enacted (overdosing of lethal drugs or poisons, slashing wrists, etc.), your speed and efficiency in notifying the appropriate community service, such as the fire or police department, will probably save a life, for these trained staffs are expertly practiced in all phases of suicide prevention. Be certain to write down accurately the victim's name, address, phone number, and type of suicide attempt. Double-check this information so the rescue team can reach the spot and take action as quickly as possible. In the meanwhile, you may be able to secure the would-be suicide's cooperation for even more immediate first aid. As bizarre as it sounds, people apparently bent on self-destruction have been known to follow careful directions for self-treatment, even when given over the phone. Warm salt water is an effective emetic to rid the patient of an overdose. Of course acids ought never be vomited; in these cases the suicide prevention team you've notified will administer the proper medication. Most poisons are packaged with clearly printed directions for emergency treatment, should the poison be taken internally. If necessary, you should try to avail yourself of these directions. In the case of bleeding, the patient can often be persuaded to apply a tourniquet or pressure point until help arrives. In all cases, the patient should be kept in communication; he should never be left on his own to wait for help. If you yourself cannot be with him, perhaps you can arrange for a relative, a friend, a minister, or another counselor to contribute the personalized support and help he needs. Often a light meal and nurturing companionship are necessary follow-ups in this kind of emergency.

If the call for help is from a person who threatens suicide or wants to talk a great deal about suicide, you must use your active listening skills to understand his particular problem or attitude which has triggered this frame of mind and emotion.

In talking with a person about his suicidal intention, you may find him confused and uncentered. Often such a person has a difficult time defining any one particular problem or evaluating his priorities among his needs. Perhaps mixed in with fears of losing a job or a mate are concerns about which movie is worth seeing, or which color bathrobe is the prettiest. His emotions pull him in every direction. He may be angry, blaming and vengeful. You can help by aiding him to clarify his emotional stance and by urging him toward a logical line of problem identification and problem solving. Or perhaps you can awaken him to alternatives which have not hitherto been apparent.

Early in the interview the counselor must be certain to learn not only the client's name and address, but other important information which might be of use ultimately, such as his place of employment, his employer's name, names of relatives, friends, or a clergyman. *Without seeming to pry*, the counselor should build a picture of the client's life and interpersonal relationships, so that every resource possible can be used in problem solving or supplying necessary emotional support.

The counselor's next task is to evaluate the subject's potential sucidal action. As a nonprofessional "people-helper" you cannot be expected to make a professional analysis, but you may find yourself in a position where you are forced to judge the seriousness of the suicide threat which is communicated to you. All such threats are certainly not of equal lethal danger. No one can evaluate these with precise accuracy, but some directors of emergency centers have devised a kind of rating scale to help their workers assess the telephone caller's intention to kill himself.

Most serious is the threat due to a feeling of absolute hopelessness in the life situation—lack of home, job, income, friends, or loved one; loss of prestige or status; loss of health; threat of prosecution, criminal involvement, or exposure. Any situation which precipitates stress, not from society's point of view but from the patient's point of view, may prompt the patient to seek escape through death.

Almost as serious is the threat accompanied by neurotic or psychotic symptons—withdrawal, extreme despondence, apathy, loss of appetite, insomnia, psychosis, agitation. Psychotic states will be characterized by delusions, hallucinations, loss of contact, or disorientation, or highly unusual ideas and experiences. Agitated states will show tension, anxiety, guilt, shame, poor impulse control, and feelings of rage, anger, hostility, and revenge. Most significant is the person's feeling that he is unable to tolerate the pressure of his emotional state.

Age and sex play an important part in suicide statistics. The rate rises with increasing age and men are more likely to kill themselves than are women. Furthermore, repeated attempts usually indicate determination for self-destruction.

Also, the suicide plan itself is important. In fact some therapists claim it is the most important clue to the final outcome of the suicide threat. The threat which gives details as to time and place and method must be taken seriously, no matter how unlikely the plan may seem. Of course a plan which is near completion is the most lethal. Planning to purchase a gun is one thing; a gun already purchased is quite something else. In addition, the seriousness of the suicidal risk rises remarkably if the person talks about other final details, such as having had his will changed, writing farewell notes, and putting his affairs in order in general.

In addition to the patient's own behavior, there are certain environmental influences which reduce or increase the risk of lethality. If the patient is in communication with family and friends, if he has a good job which affords him self-esteem, if he has the kind of counseling he needs, the patient is not as likely to take his own life as he might be if these supports did not exist. The general attitude of his family is also important. If they seem secretive and ashamed of the patient's condition, he will feel the stress of their lack of acceptance. But if they are empathetic and concerned, such stress usually subsides.

It is wise for the counselor to share the responsibility and care of the patient with as many "caring" persons as possible, so that the potential suicide feels a broad, firm support. The counselor should be able to discuss the patient's problems openly with the family and perhaps also a clergyman and family physician. Encircled by supportive people, the patient can combat the sense of alienation which so often underlies the suicide attempt. Most important in this circle of support is the "significant other," that person most valued in the patient's environment. If the significant other is non-helpful, that is, if he tries to deny the patient's suicidal tendencies, or if he is unresponsive to the patient's emotional needs, the suicide risk rises critically. Of course, if the significant other is sensitive and understanding, neither too anxious nor too casual, the risk is reduced.

Another factor which has a bearing on the risk evaluation is the patient's physical health. Pain is exhausting and demoralizing, and fear of death is debilitating emotionally. Some potential suicides suffer from ungrounded fears, but the torment is just as persistent as in cases showing a clinical diagnosis of fatal illness. The relationship with the physician usually has, in these cases, a significant bearing upon the patients' mental health. They must be under the care of doctors they can trust and who will expend the time and patience to reassure and counsel them.

Because no one can academically chart and evaluate forewarning of self-destruction with any degree of precision, it is dangerous to rely too heavily on any arbitrary rating scale. Homosexuals, alcoholics, and drug addicts tend to be high suicidal risks; however, you must consider each person individually, taking into consideration all conditions which might influence his true emotional state.

You must also take into consideration the degree of rapport you yourself have been able to build with the person who calls for help. More than in any kind of counseling, the effectiveness of crisis counseling depends very much upon a chemistry of personal interaction.

Once you have made some kind of evaluation, you must have a follow-through plan of action. This plan will depend not only upon the basic suicide potential, but also upon the progress made during the interview. The counselor asks himself, has he been able to focus the interview successfully in order to center the client's emotional and mental states? Has the client been able to respond coherently in order to see his situation realistically and to inaugurate any necessary problem solving? Has the client's mood improved perceptably during the course of the interview? Taking all these circumstances into consideration, the counselor will decide upon the disposition of the case.

If the situation appears to be out of control, the family should be notified and arrangements made for taking the client to a hospital. In these emergencies, the client should not be left alone but should always be under the watchful care of a member of the family, a nurse, or counselor.

Even if there seems to be a moderate suicide risk, the suicide threat is usually a "cry for help" because of serious life problems, and the troubled person needs to be referred to some professional resource in the community. In this case, the nonprofessional counselor should make certain, without betraying any confidences, that the family or a minister or close friend is fully aware of the client's emotional instability and should also assume the moral responsibility of the potential suicide until responsibility is assumed by another resource.

In a few instances the lay counselor can safely assume that his own support and guidance has been enough to restore the suicidal person's well-being, but the nonprofessional must be careful about making such an evaluation. If no professional person is available, it is wise to enlist the continued aid of a close friend or relative of the client so as to ensure continued contact. The client should be assured of the counselor's continued help and availability.

Perhaps you puzzle over the dynamics of this ultimate in violence: self-murder. You can understand the despair of the aged, ailing derelict for whom life becomes a painful loneliness, but what about those vital, talented youths who apparently hold the world and all its promise in the palms of their hands, whose present petty problems do not seem to warrant self-inflicted death? You no doubt feel you could work more effectively if you could find a clue to the mysterious syndrome of emotions which takes root within the psyche to plot against the strong instinct for survival.

Personality theorists maintain that in many instances anger, guilt, and desire for punishment, turned both inward and outward, promote the depressive state leading to suicide. They claim that unconsciously there is within the victim a deep-seated boil of festering resentment, even while he appears outwardly to be contented and carefree. Of course every human entertains some degree of hostility, evoked by the ordinary rub of life, then subsequently feels somewhat guilty (as society teaches him to feel) and deserving of punishment for harboring such hostility. Karl Menninger points out[26] that despite our cultural pretense that "nice people are always kind and loving," in human nature "the necessity to hate is as fundamental as the necessity to love, and the two emotions are combined in our feelings for the people about us."

Though scarcely anyone is instructed in the skill of washing away these hates—feelings of betrayal, resentment, bitterness—most people stumble onto one way or another to rid themselves of aggressive emotion and accompanying guilt. They defiantly "blow their top," talk at length frankly with a close friend, express themselves in violent activities, employ psychological defenses such as rationalization or projection, or otherwise ventilate their pent-up rancor. Unfortunately, the prospective suicide often finds no outlet. Perhaps his denial of these forbidden emotions is so complete that he is not even aware they need an outlet; therefore, he himself cannot understand the great pressures that are capped and buried within a deep personal purgatory until they can no longer be contained, finally seeping out in a flow of aggression that must be turned inward because he has forbidden it to turn outward. However, inasmuch as he originally felt the hostility toward outside agencies, perhaps parents, the suicide itself may be used as a weapon of retaliation, whether he recognizes the fact or not.

Within your own experiences you have probably known such cases akin to one which was recorded some years ago. Bruce Caldwell, an intelligent, good-looking, extremely popular young bachelor, was employed by an American firm in Hong Kong, when his friends began to notice a slight personality change. Usually sociable and outgoing, he became withdrawn, forgetful, apathetic.

Bruce had been hired immediately after his discharge from the army, where he had distinguished himself by his courage and leadership. In his present job also, his efficiency impressed his superiors, who considered him a valuable employee. However, his boss found it convenient to use

Bruce as a scapegoat, a role he accepted with no more protest than a shrug of the shoulders. Recently he'd also shrugged off his disappointment when he'd fallen deeply in love with a girl who, as he learned too late, was already married and whose religion forebade divorce.

When Bruce's parents had visited Hong Kong sometime previously, everyone was impressed by the mutual familial devotion. At expense he could not afford, Bruce had entertained his parents lavishly, while his mother had never tired of recounting what a "good" boy her son had always been: a "good" student, a "good" musician (he had taken up piano to please his mother), a "good" worker in school government, a "good" athlete—though often exhausted by his heavy schedule of activities and obligations. She especially had praised his "good" disposition. He'd never carped or complained, always smiled no matter how disconcerting a situation might be.

A few weeks after his personality change began to be apparent, Bruce quit work and returned to his parents' home in the United States. A few hours after his arrival, he quietly went to the basement and, with a single pistol shot, ended his life.

Granted that no one ever claimed to know precisely what prompted this action, Bruce's life history certainly suggests there was the combination of buried aggression and guilt which caused the eventual explosive reaction. Bruce had learned in early childhood to be a "good" boy, to perform his duty faultlessly without complaint despite the normal resentment he often must have felt. In the end he returned to the locale of much of that suppressed hostility and guilt in order to enact the punishment, upon himself and upon his parents.

In addition to the notion that depression is often born of buried anger, it is apparent that deep depression is often engendered by a person's feeling that he has lost control of his life situation. He feels helpless and hopeless and bogs down emotionally. He may feel this way about a certain insurmountable problem, perhaps the inability to find a job, or the inability to achieve good grades no matter how much he studies, or the inability to win the love of someone very important to him. Or he may have a more undefined feeling of lack of control, just that he is, in general, not the master of his own fate. Instead, he feels that he is weak and ineffectual.

A few years ago a man came to me who'd been suffering a painful depression for several weeks. He was entangled in a complicated legal battle which was certain to drag on for months, perhaps even longer. However, as it turned out, his depression was bred not so much by the legal procedure itself as by the feeling that he was a helpless pawn being pushed around by capricious judges, ambiguous laws, and accidents of fate. He himself had no power, no control over what might happen to him.

Other cases of depression might be caused by an overwhelming, insurmountable problem, such as poor health or the loss of a loved one. Sometimes there is a depressive reaction from the use of alcohol or drugs, or there is a long-standing chronic emotional illness of unknown etiology, or even in a few rare cases, a systemic chemical imbalance. Of course this last can be determined only by a physician.

In a book entitled *Clues to Suicide*,* are a number of actual suicide notes which bear out the feelings of anger (usually somewhat concealed), hopelessness, frustration, and confusion suffered by suicidal persons. Many of the notes show the careful planning which often accompanies suicide, and also in some cases an attitude that the potential suicide is an accomplished fact.

1. I hope this is what you wanted. Signed Bill.

2. Goodbye my Dear. I am very sorry but it is just too hard to breathe. Love, Bill. Dearest, have someone at the Legion call the V.A. I think they will take care of me.

3. Somewhere in this pile is your answers. I couldn't find it. Mom, you should have known what was about to happen after I told you my troubles now I will get my rest. Dad, I am in this jam because I trusted

---

*Excerpts from *Clues to Suicide* by Edwin S. Shneidman and Norman L. Farberow. Copyright © 1957 by Edwin S. Shneidman and Normal L. Farberow. Used with permission of McGraw-Hill Book Company.

people (namely you) and some people trusted me, because I am, in my present state a menace to me and my customers I think this is the best way out and out of my insurance. If you ever take a drink I hope you drown yourself with it.

4. Dear Mary, The reason for my despondency is that you'd prefer the company of almost anyone to mine. You told me you preferred living alone. This led to more sedatives. I have lost the love of my two children. You blamed me for your vaginal bleeding. Your first husband denied normal sexual intercourse because you said it hurt. I received the same accuse. (sic) You said it hurt even out of wedlock. This you can't help. But affection would have been harmless. I had little of that. My salary wasn't enough for a large family with the car upkeep. I was happy regardless. So were you between moods also. You are free now to frequent the places where they drink and indulge in loose talk. Please refrain from giving Betty sips of beer, after all she is only 12. Make her love you some other way. Soon she'll dominate you and one thing leads to another. You don't want another child where your boy is. Your love for me would have endured if it had been the real thing. Dr. Jones did all he could for my internal trouble. When we quarrel over other and younger men it was silly but you would have been hurt too. It's OK to be friendly, but not hilarious. Nembutal has a tendency to make you tolerant rather than jealous. It headed off many a quarrel because it's quieting to the nerves. As you know I took them for sleep and spastic colon at nite; also migrane (sic) headache. Well, I've loved you through 3 years of quarreling, adjusting the sex angle the way you said it pleased you. Your word for it was "ecstasy." Farewell and good fortune. I hope you find someone who doesn't "hurt" you as you said 3 of us did. All the love I have, Bill. Notify my kin by mail. Call Georgia St. Hospital Ambulance.

5. Dear Mary; I'm just to (sic) tired and to (sic) sick of trying to continue. Sorry it had to be this way. I'm sure everything will work out for the best. Keep everything as quiet as possible. Say I had a heart attack. As ever, Bill. God forgive me. God bless you and John.

6. Dear Mary. Since you are convinced that you are an invalid and no one can help you, I hope my $3000 insurance will help you to see the truth about yourself and get rid of your mental sickness. You are now free to marry Joe. Remember you will never have any happiness with anyone until you learn to help yourself. I have no regrets and hold no malice or unkind thoughts toward you. We would have had a happy life together if you had wanted to help yourself. I hope you eventually will find happiness. Love, Bill. Tell my folks I'm sorry I couldn't see them before I went.

In this same book is found the comment,

> ...the saddest thought of all is to see the suicide as he really is, a forlorn, beaten, and deprived person who has peopled his emptiness with malefactors and villains of his own making. His small ingrown self becomes an empty cosmos peopled with his tormentors and detractors. In an immense moment of fantastic grandiosity he lays them, and all the world to ruin. But instead of leaving the world as he fantasies it, desolated and sere, stricken and laid waste by the magnitude of his act, he gains only a personal surcease from pain and a small footnote in the inside pages of a newspaper. He goes out "not with a bang but a whimper," a dupe to the irrationality within himself.

Obviously, the quote does not apply to all suicides; in certain cases all but the most heartless among us would hope that the victim could find peace and freedom from pain by whatever means available. But the author makes his point— in most instances the suicidal person sees the world through a distorted emotional lens.

In addition to depression and potential suicide, there is another type of personal crisis which you will probably encounter eventually. With the current availability of a wide variety of drugs, many users find themselves experiencing unexpected, frightening reactions. Sometimes they feel too sedated, sometimes too "high," or sometimes the user is having a "bad trip." A "bad trip" is an adverse psychological reaction to one of the hallucinogenic drugs, especially LSD. A hallucinogenic drug is one which alters the body chemistry to such an extent that one experiences mental, auditory, visual, and other sense distortions. The most common hallucinogens are LSD, psilocybin, mescaline, and DMT.

Anyone planning to be a "people-helper" should send to the Superintendent of Documents, U.S. Government Printing Office, Washington, D.C. 20402, for the federal source book entitled *Answers to the Most Frequently Asked Questions About Drug Abuse*. Interestingly, this pamphlet includes a drug users' glossary of slang. But more important, it contains a cataloguing of drugs along with descriptions of their effects, physical and mental. Not only is the pamphlet generally enlightening, but it teaches vocabulary terms and physical responses which you will then recognize in dealing with "bad trippers" or drug users in general.

There are many reasons for drug users to experience an unexpected reaction. The drug may have been adulterated in some way, or the user may have taken it in the wrong setting, or his physical or mental condition may have been maladaptive. Or he may have taken too much of the drug, or in a spirit of experiment, combined incompatible drugs.

As in all other counseling, the counselor must interact in a way to inspire trust and acceptance. At this time you are not concerned with the person's unlawful drug use or moral consequences. In the early part of the interview, you should get as much information as possible, such as name and address, without arousing distrust or agitating the person in any way, in case emergency treatment is necessary. In view of legal regulations of drug use, a telephone caller may disconnect the call if you appear too nosy or concerned about certain details. If you are handling the counseling situation in person, you can be more direct in your questions which, of course, you are asking in order to be as helpful as possible.

If the user has taken an overdose of drugs which can be pumped from the stomach, you should arrange for him to go immediately to an emergency center where the staff on duty can perform this service. In view of prevailing fears of being "busted," at times it's difficult to persuade the user to put himself in the hands of any agency he feels is representative of higher authority. He is often suspicious and frightened. As a last resort, you might persuade him to take a warm, strong salt water emetic, or even slip his finger down his throat to induce vomiting. Your exact directions for the procedure will depend upon whether the user is alone, whether he is at home or in public, or with friends, whether you are at the end of a telephone or in a counseling center, and so on.

If the user has ingested sedatives, such as barbiturates, he should be kept physically and mentally active. Black coffee will help keep him awake, as will a continuous routine of walking and conversation. He ought not be allowed to relax or go to sleep until the drug has had ample time to wear off. Even then he ought to be under observation for several hours.

If the user feels too "high" or on a "bad trip," he needs to be talked "down." It is not advisable to use a tranquilizer to counteract the "high," unless the user grows physically violent, endangering himself or others. One reason not to use a tranquilizer is that you can't be certain of the effect of combining drugs. Individuals react differently to drugs. Besides, there's really no way to know exactly what drugs the user has already taken, for "pushers" adulterate street drugs in many different ways. In any case, additional drugs for treatment purposes should be prescribed only by a physician. The counselor's job is to help the person overcome negative emotional and psychological reactions. The counselor concentrates on two objectives. For one thing, he soothes and relaxes the person. In addition, he persuades the person that he himself, not the drug, is in control of his mind and body. Both objectives are accomplished by the counselor's steady, soothing, assured talking. In order that the person be kept quiet physically and emotionally, the atmosphere of his room should be as comfortable and relaxing as possible, with perhaps some soft music along with the calming, tranquilizing voice of the counselor. Because of this need for pleasant calm and quiet, it is usually best not to take the client to an emergency center where there are likely to be bright lights, clanging of equipment, shouts, crying, the sight of blood, and an air of disaster. Instead, all sound should be low-key with all conversation centered on restful, good feelings or enjoyable memories and experiences. Perhaps the person needs to be held or caressed by someone he feels comfortable with. As in any other crisis counseling, the person should be under observation for an extended period and should be assured of the counselor's continued help and availability.

When you first think of yourself as a paraprofessional counselor, no doubt the thought of becoming involved with depressives or drug addicts may unnerve you. However, as you gain skill and experience, you will begin to feel proficient and self-assured in any crisis. Your self-confidence will be communicated to those whom you are helping and will be their greatest consolation.

One more word, a very important one. If you are to become involved in crisis counseling, you are likely to experience a tragic sense of failure and guilt should one of those persons you've counseled proceed to take his own life. However, you must remember that you are no more responsible for this death than is a medical doctor responsible for a fatal case of cancer. A virulent physical disease sometimes runs its course, ending in death despite any human intervention; a mental disease sometimes runs its course with the same finality. As any psychiatrist, psychologist, social worker, or counselor will tell you, there's no way you can prevent a person's taking his own life if he's determined to do so. You can only accept the fact that human beings are granted the gift of free will, and a few tormented persons will choose to escape the pain they feel they can no longer endure. You cannot deny them this choice. You can only hope that someday we will learn enough about the human condition so that such unbearable mental and emotional stress will not occur; or, if it does occur, everyone will have the strength and wisdom to handle it in a constructive, rather than destructive, manner.

10.

A Small Glossary of Mental Illness

If you are to be involved as a paraprofessional in a counseling center, even as a volunteer worker, you may have occasion to read the professional reports, evaluations, or case histories. Perhaps a small glossary of terms relating to mental illness would acquaint you with a few basics and some vocabulary so that such reading material will not be foreign to you. Of course, you must keep in mind the limitations of this brief encounter. Any library or college bookstore has texts on abnormal psychology; however, you may find yourself in the same position as the little girl who received as a present a very large book on the subject of cats. Later on, her mother asked her why she hadn't read the book and the little girl replied that there was more in that book than she cared to know about cats. Most abnormal psychology books are very thick and forbidding looking, containing more than most people want to know.

Mental illness is a disease characterized by inappropriate responses to the life situation. If a person is overemotional, exceedingly immature, irrational, excessively irresponsible, withdrawn, or overanxious, he is said to have a mental illness. Of course the seriousness of the illness depends upon the degree of behavioral distortion. Emotional or mental illness is not a matter of black and white in the same way as a disease caused by bacteria. A mild form of mental illness may make someone afraid of heights, while a more severe form may make another person fear that the whole world is plotting against him. In extreme cases the world may be lost completely, as with a schizophrenic who blocks out reality to live where he cannot be reached by reason. Such behavior is only the sign or symptom of mental illness. The illness itself is a basic disorder in the mental-emotional process which compels the aberrant behavior.

Some cases of mental illness are "organic." This means there has been some kind of injury to the brain, due either to head wounds or to diseases such as encephalitis or syphilis, or to drugs or alcohol, or to congenital conditions or heredity.

However, most mental illnesses are "functional," meaning they are due to psychological causes. Perhaps there has been excessive stress during childhood which has resulted in withdrawal compulsions, phobias, anxieties, low self-esteem, lack of independence or other personality "quirks." Perhaps there are economic or social pressures which present insurmountable problems and stress; such pressures implant continuous feelings of helplessness and frustration. Or perhaps there are temporary but intensive high-stress situations such as battlefront experiences, loss of a job or a loved one, or a prolonged, debilitating illness. In general, the degree of ego strength built in the early years will determine the amount of stress which the person can tolerate later in life.

Mental illness can also be a result of a combination of physical and psychological causes. Drug addiction, alcoholism, extreme obesity, and all the psychosomatic illnesses involve both the soma and the psyche, to the detriment of both.

The mental illnesses referred to here will fit into three categories: 1. *Psycho-Neuroses*, 2. *Personality Disorders*, 3. *Psychoses*.

Psycho-Neuroses

Emotional maladaptations due to unresolved unconscious conflicts...A neurosis is usually less severe than a psychosis, with minimal loss of contact with reality. Thinking and judgment may be impaired. A neurotic illness represents the attempted resolution of unconscious emotional conflicts in a manner that handicaps the effectiveness of a person in living. Types of neuroses are usually classified according to the particular symptoms which predominate.[27]

The psycho-neuroses are the most common kind of mental illness and everyone experiences some of these to a limited degree. Everyone is a little "up tight" or a little over-emotional or a little determined to control or manipulate those around him so that he'll feel more secure and comfortable. The neurotic reaction is basically a defense, a protective mechanism against the world. In its mild form it makes a person feel safer. However, as one feels more in need of protection, he may step up this defensive reaction until he begins to exaggerate or misinterpret what he sees or hears. He may grow fearful about how people respond to him, or grow hostile about imagined rejections, or develop excessive self-pity, or become overanxious about imaginary physical ailments. However, the neurotic person, unlike the psychotic, always interacts with the real world. He battles with inner conflict, and he may react in a way which is inadequate, but he never confuses the real with the completely unreal.

There are several kinds of psycho-neuroses.

Traumatic Neurosis

The term encompasses combat, occupational, and compensation neurosis. These are neurotic reactions which have been attributed to or which follow a situational traumatic event, or series of events. Usually the event has some specific and symbolic emotional significance for the patient, which may be reinforced by *secondary gain* (the external gain which is derived from any illness, e.g., personal attention and service, or monetary gains such as disability benefits).

This neurosis is precipitated by sudden catastrophe or stress, such as wartime situations on the battlefield, a major car accident, an earthquake, or other such emergency which forces the normal person to call upon his every resource to avoid being overwhelmed. The person may lose his appetite, be unable to relax, suffer insomnia or other physical symptoms.

Anxiety Reaction

Characterized primarily by direct experiencing of anxiety, which may have an acute or gradual onset, with subjective uneasiness or apprehension out of proportion to any apparent external cause. The anxiety is uncontrollable, and the utilization of various specific defense mechanisms common to other neuroses is minor.

Everybody suffers mild anxiety from time to time. It may be connected with fear or dread, often a reluctance to face something unpleasant. Sometimes there's just a free-floating anxiety that life is not going to turn out the way a person wants it, but he can't quite put his finger on the exact reason or cause. Nevertheless, people usually feel pretty secure most of the time. However, in neurotic anxiety, the anxiety is a continuous, tormenting feeling. Tension, irritability, suspicion, or fear is present most of the time. Fear may be vague and free-floating or it may fasten upon people and events in the immediate environment. The victim may have a constant preoccupation with real or imagined physical symptoms (hypochondriasis) or he may feel an overwhelming, continual jealousy without cause. Physical symptoms may include sweating, diarrhea, apprehension, breathlessness, headache, tightness in the chest, and so on. Acute attacks may last as short as a few minutes or be prolonged for weeks or months.

Depressive Reaction

A general term covering various types of neurotic depressive reactions in which insight is impaired but not so severely as in a psychotic depression.

Most people have suffered at least temporary spells of mild depression. They get discouraged or suffer setbacks or feelings of rejection. However, they "snap out of it," as the saying goes, and feel fairly optimistic for the most part. On the other hand, neurotic depression is prolonged depression that goes beyond any reasonable cause. Even if generated by some disappointment or loss, it is out of proportion to the event which triggered it. Among the symptoms are despondency, lack of activity, diminished interest, the inability to work or concentrate, and lack of self-assurance. Very often the depressed person feels abused and unloved. Psychologists generally agree that depression often covers up another emotion, such as hostility, guilt, or a feeling of being out of control of one's own life situation.

Conversion Reaction (Somatic Conversion)

> A reaction in which unacceptable unconscious impulses are converted into bodily symptoms. Instead of being experienced consciously, the emotional conflict is expressed by physical symptoms.

Known also as hysteria, this is a neurotic condition in which physical symptoms appear without any identifiable organic cause. In effect, the mind prevents anxiety from being expressed by the usual route, the emotional outlet. Instead, the mind represses the conflicts or traumas and then converts them into physical symptoms, which are functional rather than organic. The patient may suffer sensory disabilities, motor disabilities, or visceral disturbances. He may develop twitches, spasms, or hiccoughing. He may suffer blindness, seizures, convulsions, loss of voice, the inability to stand or walk, all without conclusive medical evidence. Although the symptoms frequently disappear when the patient is asleep or under hypnosis, the symptoms are real and not faked; the patients are sincere in their descriptions of suffering and malfunction. They agree to radical surgery if informed that such intervention is needed. In some situations the affliction seems appropriate to the underlying anxiety. A long-distance runner who fears he will lose an important race may suffer paralysis of the legs; or a seamstress who sees her work as unfulfilling and dull may suffer a disability which deprives her of the use of her hands. Difficult to explain is the fact that while mental health problems are generally on the upward swing, cases of hysteria are growing more rare.

Dissociative Reaction

A reaction characterized by such dissociated behavior as amnesia, fugues, sleepwalking, and dream states.

Dissociative reaction involves a number of neurotic conditions where a disturbance of consciousness occurs. Some of these are sleepwalking, amnesia, and multiple personality. In each case, the patient successfully blocks off part of his life from conscious recognition, thereby defending his ego structure. The sleepwalker has his eyes open and knows where he is going but believes himself to be dreaming. The amnesia patient cannot recall his name, address, or past circumstances, but his basic habit patterns remain intact. Amnesia is sometimes accompanied by a "fugue" state, a literal flight from familiar surroundings and way of life. Movie and TV scripts have made much of the hero who turns up far from home, unable to recall any previous identity or experience. Multiple personality cases are rare conditions where separate personalities exist in the same person; such a separation allows the emergence of traits which would ordinarily be hidden. Inasmuch as this condition is dramatic and fascinating, the few case histories on file have received more than their share of attention and publicity. Probably everyone has heard of *The Three Faces of Eve* and *Sybil*. In each case, the patient seems to be not one person but several, each with its own appearance, personality, and role. For instance, Eve was sometimes Eve White—dignified, industrious, conservative, pathetic. At times she was Eve Black—seductive, mirthful, mischievous, carefree. Later she was Jane—wholesome, mature, capable. Eventually, after long therapy, a new personality emerged, much like Jane but more complete and authentic.

Phobic Reaction

A reaction characterized by a continuing, specific irrational fear out of proportion to apparent stimuli. . . .The fear is believed to arise through a process of displacing an internal (unconscious) conflict to an external object symbolically related to conflict . . .

Phobias are neurotic states involving irrational, unreasonable fear of some situation or object. A few of these fears are somewhat shared by most people, such as fear of snakes, or of the dark, but phobic persons suffer the fear much more acutely, exaggerating the threat or danger. Other phobias, such as fear of open spaces or of cats, are rarely shared even mildly by the average person. Some of the more common phobias are: Acrophobia—fear of high places, Agoraphobia—fear of open places, Claustrophobia—fear of closed places, Mysophobia—fear of germs, Thanatophobia—fear of death. It is believed that most phobias allow the individual to circumscribe his conflicts and anxieties, therefore limiting them to a definable and controllable situation. This outward fear may mask an inner fear he dares not face. Of course phobias are sometimes learned. A mother who fears cats may teach her children, by example, the same—Aleurophobia.

Obsessive Compulsive Reaction

Reaction patterns associated with the intrusion of insistent, repetitive, and unwanted ideas, or of repetitive, unwelcome impulses to perform certain acts. The afflicted person may feel compelled to carry out rituals such as repeated hand-washing, touching, or counting.

Obsessive-compulsive neurosis involves the repetitions of thoughts (obsessions) or actions (compulsions) which seem to enter the mind unbidden. Everyone has experienced this to a mild degree. A melody will obsessively haunt a person, repeating itself over and over in his mind. Or a person will feel compelled to straighten a crooked picture or pick up a bit of lint from the floor or doodle as he is talking on the phone. But the severely neurotic obsessive-compulsive victim may find his life has become a nightmare. He may wash his hands so many times that he wears the skin raw, or he may not be able to work as a salesperson because he is obsessed by a certain number and cannot make change when this figure is involved, but must repeat the number over and over again, or perhaps must always avoid this number and leave it out entirely. Even when obsessive ideas and compulsive behaviors are resisted, they are a source of anxiety and torment to the patient. If not resisted, they may take up much of the patient's time and energy. Perhaps the patient is blocking out certain anxieties by giving himself over to diverting, irrelevant ideas and acts. Or perhaps the patient is driven by a neurotic anxiety to feel in control of his world, putting everything about him in perfect order and alignment.

Hypochondriasis

Persistent overconcern with the state of physical or emotional health accompanied by various bodily complaints without demonstrable organic pathology.

Hypochondriasis is a neurotic condition characterized by an exaggerated concern for one's physical health. Preoccupation with the body and its functions occupy much of the patient's time. Usually the hypochondriac is maladapted socially, with low self-esteem and fear of close interpersonal relationships. His genuine anxiety concerning his aches and pains consumes most of his energies and forestalls any efforts at socialization which, in the past, have usually led to disappointment anyway.

Personality Disorders

A generic term denoting those mental conditions in which the basic disorder lies in the personality of the individual. There is minimal subjective anxiety and little or no sense of distress.

Personality disorders are not classified as neuroses. Their outstanding characteristic is a marked lack of adjustment to society and to the realities of everyday life. Loss of one or both parents, deprived early environment, racial prejudice, lack of parental love, or other unhealthy early influence are often associated with subsequent personality disorders.

Antisocial Personality

A person whose behavior is predominately amoral or antisocial and characterized by impulsive, irresponsible actions satisfying immediate and narcissistic interests without concern for obvious and implicit social consequences accompanied by minimal outward evidence of anxiety or guilt.

Antisocial personality was at one time termed "psychopathic personality" and this term is often still used. Although typically intelligent, spontaneous, and very likable on first acquaintance, a person of this type is soon found to be irresponsible, emotionally immature, and totally without conscience. He lacks any show of anxiety or guilt, even when found guilty of rape or murder. He lives completely for his own self-centered enjoyment and takes what he wants from the world. Lacking a conscience, he is highly resistant to rehabilitation.

Passive-Aggressive Personality

Characterized by aggressive behavior exhibited in passive ways, such as pouting stubbornness, procrastination, and obstructionism.

The passive-aggressive personality's most outstanding characteristic is his dependency. Outwardly eager to please people, he hides a morbid resentment which sometimes explodes. He is often socially skillful and manipulative.

Compulsive Personality

A personality characterized by excessive adherence to rigid standards. Typically the individual is inflexible, overconscientious, overinhibited, unable to relax, and exhibits repetitive patterns of behavior.

The compulsive personality is rigid and overinhibited. He is

overconscientious and constantly aware of rules and regulations and standards, especially of a moral nature. He is overly
conforming and finds it difficult to relax. He tends to be a
perfectionist.

Explosive Personality

> This behavior pattern is characterized by gross outbursts of rage or of
> verbal or physical aggressiveness. . . . These patients are generally
> considered excitable, aggressive and overresponsive to environmental
> pressures. It is the intensity of the outbursts and the individual's
> inability to control them which distinguishes this group...

The explosive personality uses anger as a weapon and as a
release for emotion.

Hysterical Personality

> These behavior patterns are characterized by excitability, emotional
> instability, overreactivity, and self-dramatization. This self-dramati-
> zation is always attention-seeking and often seductive, whether or not
> the patient is aware of its purpose. These personalities are also
> immature, self-centered, often vain, and usually dependent on others.

The hysterical personality is overemotional, dramatic, ex-
citable, immature, and romantic. Often persons of this type
have difficulty handling the realities of a marital relationship,
expecting the marriage partner to be ever-romantic, flattering and seductive, as though on a never-ending
honeymoon.

Paranoid Personality

> This behavior pattern is characterized by hypersensitivity, rigidity,
> unwarranted suspicion, jealousy, envy, excessive self-importance, and
> a tendency to blame others and ascribe evil motives to them.

The paranoid personality somewhat resembles the more
emotionally disturbed paranoid-schizophrenic. Like the more
seriously ill person, he is suspicious, and often feels exploited
and rejected. He is usually jealous and hostile, feeling the
whole world is against him.

Cyclothymic Personality (Affective Personality)

This behavior pattern is manifested by recurring and alternating periods of depression and elation. Periods of elation may be marked by ambition, warmth, enthusiasm, optimism, and high energy. Periods of depression may be marked by worry, pessimism, low energy, and a sense of futility. These mood variations are not readily attributable to external circumstances.

We have all known people who always seem to be either "on top" or else the opposite—suffering a case of "the blues." Usually we just refer to them as moody and realize that we never know from one day to the next whether they'll be good company or not.

Schizoid Personality

This behavior pattern manifests shyness, oversensitivity, seclusiveness, avoidance of close or competitive relationships, and often eccentricity. Autistic thinking without loss of capacity to recognize reality is common, as is daydreaming and the inability to express hostility and ordinary aggressive feelings. These patients react to disturbing experiences and conflicts with apparent detachment.

These people are often referred to by their friends as "loners," "introverts," or "daydreamers."

Sexual Deviations

This category is for individuals whose sexual interests are directed primarily toward objects other than people of the opposite sex, toward sexual acts not usually associated with coitus, or toward coitus performed under bizarre circumstances as in necrophilia (abnormal excitement in the presence of corpses), pedophilia, sexual sadism, and fetishism. Even though many find their practices distasteful, they remain unable to substitute normal sexual behavior for them.

Fetishism Process of attachment of special meaning to an inanimate object (or fetish) which serves, usually unconsciously, for the original object or person. The substitute object is often a neurotic source of sexual stimulation or gratification.

Pedophilia   Erotic attachment to small children.

Transvestitism   Sexual pleasure derived from dressing or masquerading in the clothing of the opposite sex.

Exhibitionism   Psychiatrically, compulsive body exposure, usually of the male genitals to females in socially unacceptable situations. Sexual stimulation or gratification usually accompanies the act.

Voyeurism   Sexually motivated and often compulsive interest in watching or looking at others, particularly at genitals. Roughly synonymous with "peeping Tom." Observed predominantly in males.

Sadism   Pleasure derived from inflicting physical or psychological pain on others.

Masochism   Pleasure derived from physical or psychological pain inflicted by oneself or by others. . . .It is the converse of *sadism* and the two tend to co-exist in the same individual.

Sexual Orientation Disturbance   An official diagnostic category for individuals whose sexual interests are directed primarily toward persons of the same sex and who...wish to change their sexual orientation.

Satyriasis   (applied to men) and

Nymphomania   (applied to women) Abnormal, insatiable sex desire and an obsession with all aspects of sex.

A continuing pattern of retarded social development is found to run throughout the sexual pathologies. Whereas most persons mature naturally through satisfactory contacts with the opposite sex, the deviant has never developed the confidence to interact with others. Strong feelings of personal inadequacy and unattractiveness compound his fear of being humiliated in normal sexual relationships.

Addiction

> Strong emotional and/or psychological dependence upon a substance, such as alcohol or a drug, which has progressed beyond voluntary control.

Addiction may be psychological or both psychological and physiological. The drug user becomes dependent upon the drug for a sense of well-being. Addicts are usually unsuccessful persons who lack confidence and self-esteem. The drug is an escape from the pain of frustrations, boredom, loneliness, or failure. The drug user, often a "loner," has not learned to accept the challenges and realities of life. The alcoholic, usually very dependent upon people, is often socially skillful and known as a "great guy." He tends to associate drinking with conviviality and social acceptance.

Psychosis

A major mental disorder of organic and/or emotional origin in which there is a departure from normal patterns of thinking, feeling, and acting. Commonly characterized by loss of contact with reality, distortion of perception, regressive behavior and attitudes, diminished control of elementary impulses and desires, abnormal mental content including delusions and hallucinations. Chronic and generalized personality deterioration may occur. A majority of patients in public mental hospitals are psychotic.

The term insane is sometimes used in reference to psychotic patients. However, insanity is a legal and social term rather than a medical one, and refers to those persons who are judged by society as unable to manage their affairs or to be held accountable for the safety of themselves or others. In psychotic disorders there is severe personality decompensation. The patient may suffer delusions (fallacious ideas held in spite of all evidence to demonstrate their error) or hallucinations (the perception of what has no basis in sensory stimulation), or behave in other ways which demonstrate his inability to distinguish the real world from the world of imagination. Because psychosis may originate from either organic brain pathology or psychological stress, psychotic disorders are divided into two groups: organic psychoses and functional psychoses.

Organic Psychoses

Serious psychiatric disorder resulting from a demonstrable physical disturbance of brain function such as a tumor, infection, or injury.

Characterized by impaired memory, orientation, intelligence, judgment, and mood.

Disorders of an organic nature include brain damage resulting from infectious diseases, vitamin or endocrine deficiency, poisonous agents, physical injury to the brain, cancerous growths, and deterioration associated with aging.

Functional Psychoses

Schizophrenia

This large category includes a group of disorders manifested by characteristic disturbances of thinking and mood behavior. Disturbances in thinking are marked by alterations of concept formation which may lead to misinterpretation of reality and sometimes to delusions and hallucinations, which frequently appear psychologically self-protective. Corollary mood changes include ambivalent, constricted and inappropriate emotional responsiveness and loss of empathy with others. Behavior may be withdrawn, regressive and bizarre. The schizoprenias, in which the mental status is attributable primarily to a *thought* disorder, are to be distinguished from the Major affective illnesses which are dominated by a *mood* disorder. The Paranoid states are distinguished from schizophrenia by the narrowness of their distortions of reality and by the absence of other psychotic symptoms.

The most common of the psychoses is termed schizophrenia (split personality) because the illness is marked by a shattering and disintegration of the personality structure. Withdrawn and emotionally blunted, the patients live in their own private worlds. There are five main types of schizophrenia.

Schizophrenia, simple type

This psychosis is characterized chiefly by a slow and insidious reduction of external attachments and interests and by apathy and indifference leading to impoverishment of interpersonal relations, mental deterioration, and adjustment on a lower level of functioning.

Simple schizophrenics are apathetic and indifferent. Blocking off personal relationships, they often neglect their personal appearance and hygiene. Usually they do not suffer delusions or hallucinations.

Schizophrenia, hebephrenic type

This psychosis is characterized by disorganized thinking, shallow and inappropriate affect, unpredictable giggling, silly and regressive behavior and mannerisms, and frequent hypochondriacal complaints. Delusions and hallucinations, if present, are transient and not well organized.

Now a rare condition although once quite common. Hebephrenics display inappropriate emotional responses, especially giggling and silliness. They suffer severe personality decompensation and give up any attempt to cope with their condition. Their delusions and hallucinations are often bizarre. Speech is incoherent with much nonsensical repetition of words and phrases.

Schizophrenia, catatonic type (two subtypes, excited and withdrawn)

It is frequently possible and useful to distinguish two subtypes of catatonic schizophrenia. One is marked by excessive and sometimes violent motor activity and excitement and the other by generalized inhibition manifested by stupor, mutism, negativism, or waxy flexibility. In time, some cases deteriorate to a vegetable state.

Catatonic schizophrenia is characterized by either stupor or uncontrolled activity. In catatonic trance, patients refuse to move, dress, or eat, remaining silent and statue-like for long periods of time. While they appear to be in trance, they probably do notice what's going on around them. Patients in catatonic excitement, on the other hand, are aggressive, hostile, and destructive. They make faces, contort their bodies and rave wildly.

Schizophrenia, paranoid type

This type of schizophrenia is characterized primarily by the presence of persecutory or grandiose delusions, often associated with hallucinations. Excessive religiosity is sometimes seen. The patient's attitude is frequently hostile and aggressive, and his behavior tends to be consistent with his delusions. In general the disorder does not manifest the gross personality disorganization of the hebephrenic and catatonic types, perhaps because the patient uses the mechanism of projection, which ascribes to others characteristics he cannot accept in himself. Three subtypes of the disorder may sometimes be differentiated, depending on the predominant symptoms: hostile, grandiose, and hallucinatory.

A patient suffering paranoid schizophrenia experiences delusions of grandeur, persecutions, or both. He attempts to cope with the world by blaming his "enemies," but personal decomposition is often severe, so that his delusions are not well systemized. He is usually hostile and suspicious.

Schizophrenia, childhood type

This category is for cases in which schizophrenic symptoms appear before puberty. The condition may be manifested by autistic, atypical, and withdrawn behavior; failure to develop identity separate from the mother's; and general unevenness, gross immaturity and inadequacy in development. These developmental defects may result in mental retardation. . .

Childhood schizophrenia is often marked by withdrawal and autism (absorption in fantasy). The child is rigid in his habits of play, often spending hours rocking or repeating other bizarre motor behavior. Usually he has experienced poor physical health from birth and is slow in all his developmental steps, perhaps never learning to talk. The parent-child relationship is abnormal; the child may refuse the relationship or, in other cases, (called symbiotic psychosis) he cannot separate himself from his mother. He is anxiety-ridden, often displaying great outbursts of hostility.

Major Affective Disorders (Affective Psychoses)

This group of psychoses is characterized by a single disorder of mood, either extreme depression or elation, that dominates the mental life of the patient and is responsible for whatever loss of contact he has with his environment. The onset of mood does not seem to be related directly to a precipitating life experience...

As stated, an affective disorder is characterized by a severe disorder of mood or emotional feelings. Two outstanding categories will be presented here:

Involutional Melancholia

This is a disorder occurring in the involutional period and characterized by worry, anxiety, agitation, and severe insomnia. Feelings of guilt and somatic preoccupations are frequently present and may be of delusional proportions. . . . .

The involutional period in life is that period when the aging process begins to make itself felt, called the climacteric (change of life). Involutional psychosis is caused by an overreaction to the fears and stresses of this critical time. A person may fear getting old or not being able to work or being lonely or dying or losing sexual power. He may feel he has failed to reach any important goal in life. This psychosis is characterized by depression and sometimes paranoid delusions.

Manic-Depressive Illnesses (Manic-Depressive Psychoses)

These disorders are marked by severe mood swings and a tendency to remission and recurrence. Patients may be given this diagnosis in the absence of a previous history of affective psychosis if there is no obvious precipitating event.

Manic-depressive psychosis is characterized by exaggerated mood swings from excessive elation to deep depression. In the manic state the patient is like a motor running at high speed. Unable to sleep he performs tirelessly, enjoys great appetite, and is in a highly elated, jovial mood. His overactivity is obvious in his speech, work, or whatever else he is doing. In his depressed underactive state, the opposite obtains. The mood change may be sudden, or it may take months to accomplish the full swing. Each mood may last an extended period or only briefly; the contrast of moods may be extreme, or there may be periods of apparent normalcy. In some cases there may be poorly systemized delusions and hallucinations.

With so many definitions of emotional illness, you may begin to wonder what definition has been given the mentally healthy person. Much has been written about the well adjusted person's typical behavior—his flexibility, self-esteem, appropriate responses, problem-solving efficiency, and so on. But Kenneth E. Appel, a past president of the American Psychiatric Association, has stated the profile clearly and succinctly. He considers the sound person as having the ability

. . . to meet and handle problems; to make choices and decisions; to find satisfaction in accepting tasks; to do jobs without avoiding them and without pushing them onto others; to carry on without undue dependency on others; to live effectively and satisfactorily with others without crippling complications; to contribute one's share to life; to enjoy life and to be able to love and be loved.[28]

Epilogue
Hail and Farewell

We began our lessons with a treatise on Acceptance. Let us end on the same note.

If everyone could find it in his heart to accept himself and to accept others, totally and unconditionally, we could throw the whole book away. Nothing is more curative than acceptance. Nothing is more loving, more joyous. Acceptance takes away fear, hate, and ugliness, leaving self-esteem in their place. Acceptance is constructive and creative.

Acceptance is the most godlike attribute to be found in the human race.

Notes

1. Of course "people-helpers" learn a lot about themselves in the course of learning the principles of helping others; any insights into human behavior can be applied both ways.
2. In case you're wondering how the story turned out, an American Naval Officer rescued me with an explosive command to the rickshaw boys and a "My God, what are you doing here?" to me. He then escorted me to a telephone.
3. Virginia Axline, *Dibs: In Search of Self*, (New York: Ballantine Books, 1972).
4. John Winburg and Wm. Wilmot, *The Personal Communication Process*, (New York: John Wiley and Sons, Inc., 1973).
5. Carl R. Rogers and Barry Stevens, *Person to Person*, (New York: Pocket Books, 1974).
6. Perhaps pedantic educationists or psychologists or semanticists would want to split hairs about the shadings of differences between the words "goals," "needs," and "objectives." I don't believe those shadings mean a thing to most of us. I use all three words in order to cover the field.
7. For any reader who has not yet had a chance to hear this old Irish joke: In an Irish pub, a man complained to Bridget, the barmaid, "There's a

mouse in my beer." So Bridget, with exaggerated politeness, calmly reached into his mug, removed the drowned varmint, and turned to leave. But the customer stopped her. "Here, you! Just come back and take this beer away!" Whereupon Bridget stormed indignantly, "Sure, what's the fuss! First you didn't want the mouse *in* your beer; now, you don't want the mouse *out* of your beer. Lord a'mighty, there's no pleasin' you!"

8. Unlike the spontaneous daydream, this directed daydream is disciplined by a predetermined story line which has been created to serve a psychological purpose.

9. Robert Ornstein, *Psychology of Consciousness*, (New York: Viking Press, 1973).

10. Alex F. Osborn, Ph.M., *Applied Imagination*, (New York: Charles Scribner's Sons, 1953).

11. Roberto Assagioli, M.D., *Psychosynthesis*, (New York: Viking Press, 1965).

12. Rollo May, *Love and Will*, (New York: Norton and Co., 1969).

13. When Polaroid Corporation announced its first color camera some years ago, the company's publicity department described the process of discovery, a creative technique which Edwin Land had taught his scientists, i.e., to visualize during moments of relaxation new molecular arrangements. After an engineer had one of these creative insights, he was able to describe it to the others so they could all visualize it, know it existed, and put it into operation.

14. The directed daydream is used in many ways for many purposes. Psychotherapists such as Robert DeSoile used it as a tool for both diagnosis and therapy, relying heavily upon the interpretation of symbols and also upon the techniques of behavior modification.

15. David Bakan, *Disease, Pain and Sacrifice: Toward a Psychology of Suffering*, (Boston: Beacon Press, 1971).

16. Rollo May, *Love and Will*.

17. Gardner Murphy, *Historical Introduction to Modern Psychology*, (New York: Harcourt, Brace and World, 1949).

18. Alfred Adler, *Understanding Human Nature*, (New York: Fawcett Publication, Inc., 1969).

19. Philip Roth, *Portnoy's Complaint*, (New York: Random House, 1967).

20. Vance Packard, *Hidden Persuaders*, (New York: Pocket Books, 1961).

21. Eric Berne, M.D., *What Do You Say after You Say Hello?* (New York: Grove Press, 1972).

22. Muriel James and Dorothy Jongward, *Born to Win: Transactual Analysis with Gestalt Experiments*. (Reading, Mass.: Addison-Wesley Publishing Company, 1971).

23. Some theorists believe that even as far back as the intrauterine stage a baby is subliminally aware of maternal attitudes and may be affected by poor emotional climate.

24. Excerpted from an interview appearing in *New York Times Magazine*, March 28, 1971.

25. Plato, *Symposium*.

26. Karl Menninger, *Man Against Himself*, (New York: Harcourt, Brace, and World, 1938).
27. The quoted definitions appearing here have been prepared and published by the American Psychiatric Association.
28. Kenneth E. Appel, "Mental Health and Mental Illness," *Social Work Yearbook*, (New York: National Association of Social Workers, 1957).